MAKING
GEORGIAN
DOLLS' HOUSES

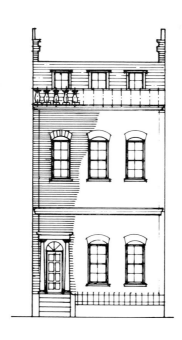

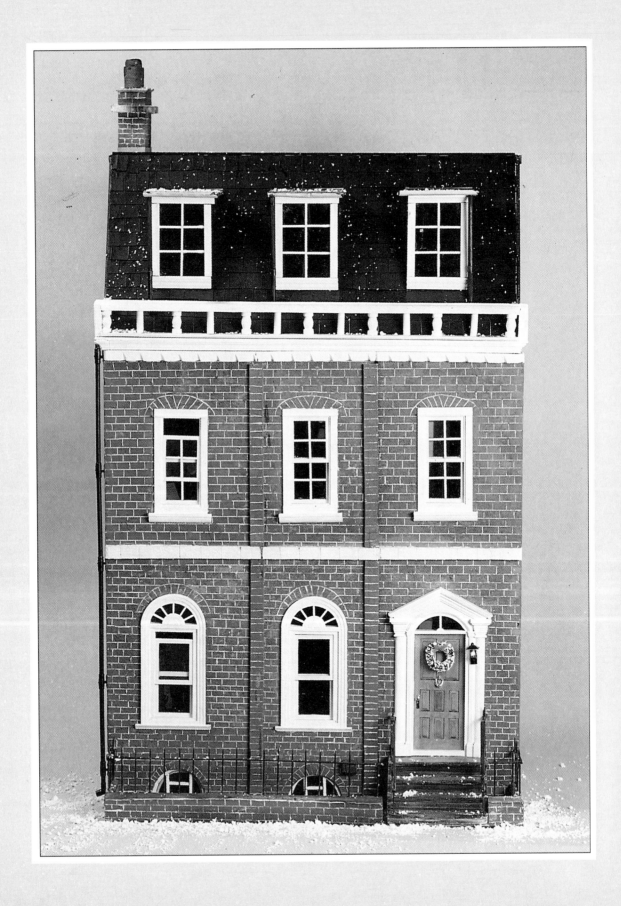

MAKING
GEORGIAN
DOLLS' HOUSES

DEREK ROWBOTTOM

GUILD OF MASTER CRAFTSMAN PUBLICATIONS LTD

First Published in 1992 by
Guild of Master Craftsman Publications Ltd,
Castle Place, 166 High Street, Lewes, East Sussex BN7 1XU

Reprinted 1994

© Derek Rowbottom 1992

ISBN 0 946819 28 9

Photography by Brian Jones, with the exceptions of the
photographs on pages 2-6 by Ian Keary

Illustrations by Robert F. Brien

Designed by Ian Hunt Design

Typeset by CST Eastbourne
Printed in Great Britain by Hillman Printers (Frome) Ltd.

I DEDICATE THIS BOOK TO
SHEILA AND MARGARET

CONTENTS

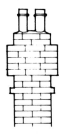 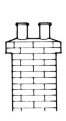 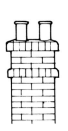 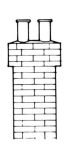 

INTRODUCTION

THIS, MY SECOND BOOK on building dolls' houses, deals pretty well exclusively with Georgian and Regency architectural styles. While these styles are often considered to be one and the same, a considerable time was to elapse after the establishment of 'Georgian' houses before 'Regency' made an appearance, though once established, the Regency features of columned door porches and multi-paned and sash windows remained in evidence well into the reign of Victoria.

Georgian houses began to appear early in the first George's reign in the early 1700s (not always the case with architecture named after monarchs), substantially replacing the wood frame house building of the Medieval and subsequent periods. Many houses built as far back as the 1650s had their plain, somewhat austere frontages faced with stone slabs or, if the owners were not too wealthy, cemented over or stuccoed to make them look new and Georgian. Many of these houses had Roman-type pillars and ornate ironwork balconies added to them (the interiors, however, remained much as they always had), and the popularity of this attractive Georgian style was established.

Regency houses used much the same methods of building, and in general the interior design and layout remained very similar to the Georgian style, particularly in town houses. These houses were largely terraced and, including the basement (usually the kitchen), would consist of four to six floors, the garret being the servants' sleeping quarters. The staircases, one above the other, would usually be located on one side of the house – general layouts of this kind of house are to be found later in the book.

Georgian and Regency houses still, thankfully, remain to be seen throughout the British Isles, from cottages and grand manor houses to farmhouses and elegant villas, all waiting to be turned into beautiful models. They have great style, and it is little wonder that the cottages and manor houses are favourites with Christmas card designers, as there is built-in charm and romantic appeal. You will not find it difficult on finishing your model to imagine it as the house of Jane Austen, or, if a town house, Dr Johnson or Beau Brummell.

This book shows how to model Georgian and Regency houses using easily obtainable materials including polystyrene sheets, composite insulating material and, of course, the indispensable plywood. The former materials are extremely easy to work, very strong and in the case of external walls, far more appropriate to the thickness of walls of the period. The all-plywood construction commonly used by kit manufacturers and suppliers of dolls' house plans is not entirely satisfactory if a high degree of scale fidelity is required in the model. For instance, as most dolls' houses are made to a $\frac{1}{12}$ scale (1″ to 1′), an exterior wall 1′ thick in a full-sized house would need to be 1″ thick in the model – the plywood supplied in kits and advised in plans is rarely thicker than $\frac{1}{8}$″! Quite apart from the cost of using 1″ plywood, the sheer weight of the finished model would also render it almost immovable, particularly a large house.

The methods of building evolved by my daughter and myself over many years are thoroughly tried and tested, and we are sure that when you have completed a house from one of the plans in this book you will agree that use of the recommended materials not only aids simplicity in construction but also has a high degree of structural strength.

A great deal of detailed work can be saved if you are prepared to purchase all the various fixtures and fittings ready-made, leaving you with only the main structure to build. A comprehensive list of stockists of these fittings can be found at the end of the book, and many of the fixtures have been incorporated into the finished models in the photographs. However, brick and floorboard papers and roof and tiling slating papers are *not* used in any of our models, as such materials have no place in the business of producing a serious model of any period of house, and really only belong in toymaking.

Ready-made items can be used as long as they are true to scale and era. For the Georgian house builder (unlike the modeller of, say, Medieval buildings), the availability of such pieces is a positive plus. However, while they will produce an excellent result, the purist will inevitably wish to model the fittings and fixtures from scratch – and if building costs are to be kept to a minimum, producing them yourself will not only reduce the costs enormously but will also provide the pleasure of having acquired a further skill.

As a modeller of many subjects, it is my opinion that the modelling of a period house can bring a satisfaction second to none. The full-sized house that we live in is, more often than not, not the one that we would choose to spend the rest of our lives in but one whose choice has been dictated by financial considerations or because it must be convenient to one's place of work, schools, etc. The building of a house in miniature, i.e. the one you would like to live in, also gives you the opportunity to furnish it with all the treasures you would like to own in the full-sized world.

Before deciding which house to build, read the book thoroughly to acquaint yourself with our methods of construction and to make yourself familiar with the finishing techniques described in detail, from wallpapers and ceilings to gutters and railings. Lighting is essential to any house interior, and even the flooring (particularly in halls, where 'marble' can be laid in a great variety of patterns) can be incorporated to good effect.

To help you make these decisions, I have included photographs of some full-sized houses at the beginning of the book, and three-view drawings for the builder with some modelling experience – by studying the plans contained in the projects together with the various construction techniques, almost any style of model house can be built. The interiors of the models contain not only mass-produced ready-made articles, but also some exquisite miniature fittings made by true craftsmen.

I would further recommend that consideration be given to the size of model you intend to build – if you already have a fair-sized collection of miniature furniture, make sure you have sufficient rooms to contain it. It is not easy to enlarge a house unless provision to do so has been made at the outset. Consider also that collecting or building furniture can become addictive, so rather than running out of house space, why not build houses as and when you need them? Enthusiasm knows no bounds.

Once all your decisions are made, curb your impatience to see it done as soon as possible, and proceed with care. Finish both interior and exterior to the best of your artistic abilities, and a great amount of pleasure and satisfaction will be yours on completion – admiration of your work will add to your sense of achievement, and you will have produced a much-cherished heirloom to be enjoyed by successive generations. And above all, enjoy the task you have set yourself!

CHAPTER ONE

DECIDING WHICH HOUSE TO MODEL

*Y*OU MAY ALREADY HAVE AN IDEA of what your ideal dolls' house will look like – if so, I hope that one of the plans in this book will meet your requirements. Even if none of them are exactly what you are looking for, I hope that, having read the book, you will find that the recommended methods of construction will enable you to produce almost any size and design of house. This book covers most of the features of Georgian architecture and photographically illustrates the often very grand styles of interior decoration developed in that period.

The Georgian period provides us with over a hundred years of history from which to draw

FIG 1.2 *Multi-paned bow windows and inset front door on a painted brick finish*

FIG 1.1 *Large brick-finished town house – note the half and quarter basement windows*

inspiration, from the reign of the first George to when Victoria ascended to the throne (the buildings of the early Victorian years were still basically Regency in style). Regency architecture in its turn differed little from the houses built in the mid-to-late Georgian era, which were constructed in a highly symmetrical manner with flat or half flat roofs, particularly in town houses. The period is of course usually identified by the addition of bow windows and similar decorative features.

FIG 1.3 *Georgian coaching
inns can provide inspiration*

We therefore have a variety of styles to choose from and can distance ourselves if we wish from the somewhat stereotyped interpretation of three floors and a flat roof so beloved of toy house builders.

As stressed in my book on Tudor dolls' houses, I would like the readers of this book to, first, produce a model, not a toy – toymaking has already been well covered in a large number of books; and second, build a model that is not simply a cabinet in which to house furniture, but one that is identifiable as a true model house of its period. It is the attention to detail that will achieve this.

The photographs clearly show that the builder has a considerable choice of styles and external finishes. My daughter and I particularly love the brick finishes of the Georgian era, especially the slightly irregular use of brick in the early Georgian period, as well as the charming variation of shades used. Such brickwork totally distinguishes these

FIG 1.4 *An imposing,
unornamented house*

houses from the later buildings of the century and from modern structures built in a neo-Georgian style. We hope to show in the chapter dealing with external finishes that the reader will find it relatively easy to build a model incorporating all the authenticity of a full-sized building.

In contrast, there are still hundreds of country houses faced with stucco, a combination of stucco and brick, or even – if in the grand style – cut stone. So your model house can range from a simple cottage to a grand town or country house with a variety of finishes, just as in the full-sized house – the choice is yours.

Consider carefully the size of house you intend to build – apart from accommodating the collection of miniatures that you may already own, plus any to be acquired in the future (collecting can become compulsive), bear in mind that building a large house can often prove easier and far less fiddly and time-consuming than building a small house.

FIG 1.5 *Note the fancy railings, decorative balustrade and stucco columns*

FIG 1.6 *Contrasting ridges of roof tiles and regular stones instead of bricks catch the eye*

If you follow the building methods we suggest, modelling a large house will result in very little extra cost, particularly if you decide to construct your own fittings and decoration.

RESEARCH

Researching which home you wish to model is a pastime in itself – great pleasure can be derived from walking around town or country and really looking at period houses with a view to producing your own scale model version. Not only can you gain inspiration, but the exercise could also prove beneficial!

FIG 1.8 *The dressed stone corners and over window decoration lighten the brickwork*

FIG 1.7 *A small whitewashed cottage with multi-pane and dormer windows*

Be sure to go equipped with a camera on these outings in case you see something to fire your imagination, and remember to try to photograph the sides and rear of houses that take your fancy. It is often the case that the owner will be only too pleased to show you the interior of the property, but these days it would be advisable to be able to prove your intentions. There is no doubt in my mind that close observation of the real thing can immensely improve both the quality and appearance of your finished model, and can help endow it with that all-important 'feel' and atmosphere.

We wish you pleasure in your building and great satisfaction with your finished model.

CHAPTER TWO

DESIGNING YOUR OWN HOUSE

*P*HOTOGRAPHS OF FULL-SIZED Georgian houses have been included in this book to inspire the modeller with some previous experience who may wish to design and build an original house. In this chapter there are also three front view drawings for further thought and, as mentioned in Chapter 1, close observation of existing Georgian houses – there will almost certainly be some in your area – can be very pleasurable and educational. I would certainly recommend this course if you intend to make up your own designs, and it is essential if you wish to correctly interpret the true colours of bricks, stucco, dressed or random stone and roof tiling and slating.

If you have decided to create an authentic one-off model, you should take as many photographs of the front, sides and back, if you mean to finish the model all round (see below). You will also need to photograph the roof and chimneys so as to model them faithfully. If you can obtain the measurements, so much the better, but if not, estimate as accurately as possible the length of the front of the building. The most commonly used scale is 1″ to 1′, and the measurements can be drawn out on 1″ square graph paper. The height of the building can now be estimated with a fair degree of accuracy, and the size of the doors and windows will be reasonably easy to work out.

The front of the model is obviously the part of the house that should be given the most attention, as it is this aspect which determines its period and character while the sides will be determined by the front. The rear of the model is not as important, as it is usually not seen, but my daughter and I believe that if the model is not finished at the back, with the same attention to detail, then the model is not really completed. And at some point you may decide to display the model in the centre of a room, thus making all the sides visible.

FIG 2.1 (A) *An imposing brick and dressed stone exterior*

FIG 2.1 (B) *A large house can take a great deal of furniture*

DESIGNING THE LAYOUT

It is common practice among model builders to take a rather large liberty when it comes to deciding how deep the finished model should be. It would seem that most full-size houses – particularly town houses – are much deeper than they are wide. Indeed, very rarely are houses less than two rooms deep, and they are often more than that, especially large Georgian, Victorian and Edwardian ones. However, compromise has to be accepted in model building – as in many other things – in the interest of producing something practical for normal usage.

A model incorporating rooms at the back of the house would be of such a size that it could not easily be shown in an average full-sized house, particularly as provision would have to be made for rear and even side openings. This would mean that there would have to be all-round access to the model, taking up even more space. The absolute purist may believe that this is the only true path to take, and certainly such a model would present many challenges, but that should not deter you – challenge is essentially what modelling is all about. With all this in mind, I have included three plan drawings of typical Georgian houses illustrating general arrangements and room positions.

Once you have produced plans to meet your requirements and all outside details have been

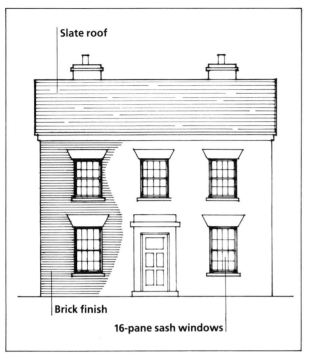

Slate roof

Brick finish

16-pane sash windows

FIG 2.2 *Late 18th/early 19th-century country house*

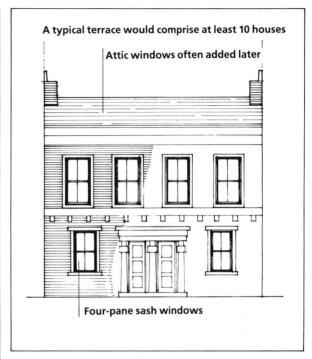

A typical terrace would comprise at least 10 houses

Attic windows often added later

Four-pane sash windows

FIG 2.3 *Two small early 19th-century terraced houses*

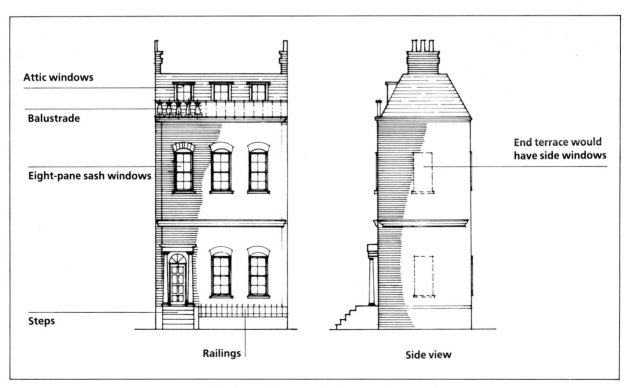

Attic windows

Balustrade

Eight-pane sash windows

Steps

Railings

End terrace would have side windows

Side view

FIG 2.4 *Early Georgian terraced or free-standing town house*

FIG 2.5 *Small two-room house*

decided, serious thought must be given to the inside layout. Some inspiration may be gained from my designs, but many variations can be arranged from these themes.

Remember to give consideration to where staircases are to be placed and where they will turn up on the next floor of your house – I have experienced the awkward situation of having a stairway coming up into a main bedroom, and this can create great difficulties. For the modeller, it is often easiest to place one staircase above another in houses of three or more storeys.

CHOOSING YOUR MATERIALS

The next step is to decide which materials to use in your model. Chapter 3, on the building materials used by my daughter and myself, covers most methods, but I would like to enlarge a little on the various materials which could be used in building from your own design.

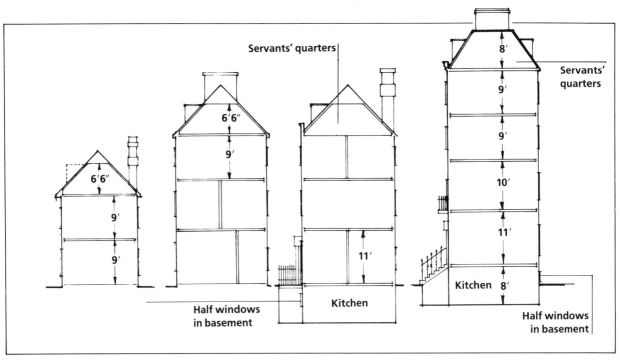

FIG 2.6 *Side elevation of small terraced house with optional attic windows*

FIG 2.7 *Side elevation of three-storey house with attic windows*

FIG 2.8 *Side elevation of terraced house with basement kitchen*

FIG 2.9 *Side elevation of large terraced house with kitchen and servants' quarters*

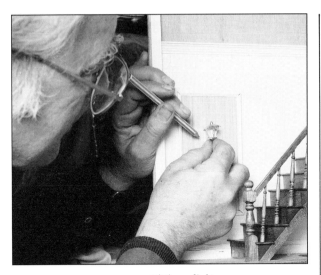

FIG 2.10 *Fitting a light*

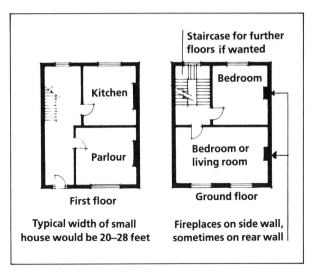

FIG 2.11 *Rooms and staircase in a small house*

The base can be of plywood, either thick – ¾″–1″ for most houses – or thin – ⅛″ framed on the underside with stripwood of ½″ × ¾″, or for larger houses ¼″ plywood framed with ¾″ × 1″ stripwood. If you use plywood, the floorboards can be simulated as described and illustrated in Chapter 5, or commercially produced flooring can be used. This is individual planks laid on a paper backing that can be glued into place.

You can also use blockboard for bases, and as this is usually ¾–1″ thick it will not require framing – if you can find knot-free facings, the floor can be finished as described above. Chipboard, cheap and readily available, can also be used, but this must be either faced on the floor surface with thin plywood – 1/16″ would be suitable – or commercial planking.

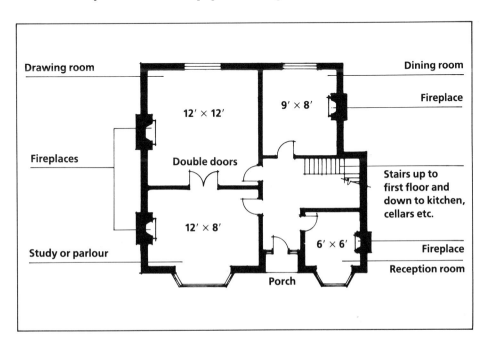

FIG 2.12 *Ground floor plan for detached house*

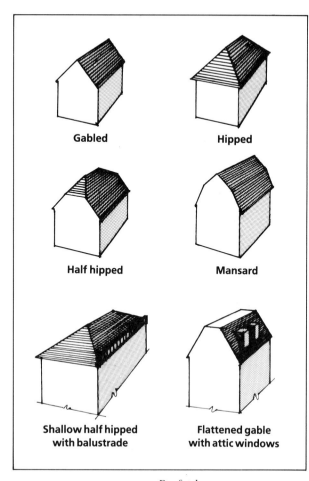

Gabled

Hipped

Half hipped

Mansard

Shallow half hipped
with balustrade

Flattened gable
with attic windows

FIG 2.13 *Roof styles*

These methods are fairly expensive, but the decision ultimately lies with you, the builder.

My daughter and I always build our models of Tudor, Stuart and Jacobean houses floor by floor, completing the ground floor before adding any others. Most houses of these periods have first floors which project over the ground floors, and in this type of building we find polystyrene foam sheet invaluable, as it has an excellent strength-to-weight ratio – useful particularly in larger houses, which can become extremely heavy if constructed entirely from wood. This foam is available from most builders' merchants. It is used as an insulating material and can be purchased in almost any thickness and in a wide variety of densities.

Methods of using this material are dealt with in detail in *Making Tudor Dolls' Houses,* and the country house in this book also makes use of polystyrene foam. It is possible to use polystyrene in the construction of the other models, but provision must be made for the extra thickness of the material. The external dimensions of a model built with polystyrene sheet will be approximately 1½″ more than the length given in the plans and about 1″ deeper. The country house plans show how to use this method, and the construction follows the floor by floor method of building.

METHODS OF CONSTRUCTION

There are still more methods of construction which can be used on their own or in various combinations. If you want to keep expenses to the minimum, hardboard can be used – it is almost indestructible and is certainly rot-proof. You can use heavy-duty cardboard, and even the corrugated variety can be considered as a building medium as it has the advantage of folded corners that could be used in the rear and side walls, which can be done in one piece. The corner has great strength when folded – just look closely at a box made to hold a vacuum cleaner or washing machine. However, as with polystyrene foam, the front edges must be edged with woodstrip to enable the front openings – which *must* be made of plywood – to be hinged. Most finishes used on plywood can be adapted for use on cardboard.

Even if your model is built of plywood or a combination of plywood and foam sheet, it is possible to use cardboard to make a fixed roof. It is easily worked, and when slated (*see* Chapter 10) it is extremely strong. However, I do not recommend it for use in roofs with attic windows.

When considering the types of material that can be employed, do not dismiss anything before experimenting a little with what is available – modelling is all about experimenting and inventing, and this is a pleasure in itself.

FIG 2.14 *Marking out with a set square*

FIG 2.15 *Exterior wall finishes*

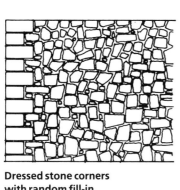

Dressed stone corners with random fill-in

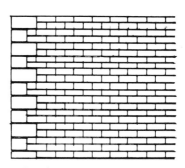

Dressed stone corners with brick

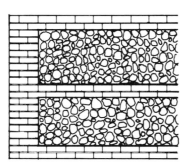

Flint walls with brick quoins and lacing courses

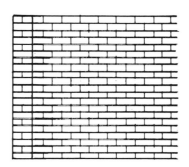

Plain brick with double brick corners

CHAPTER THREE

TOOLS

MY FATHER (who, incidentally, had little craftsmanship or artistic talent) insisted on reminding me, when exploring my talents as a schoolboy equipped with only a single-sided razorblade, a saw with teeth that were virtually non existent and a few chisels sharpened down to about 2″ from the handle, that it was a poor workman that blamed his tools! How much wisdom there was in that remark I have still to find out – however, limiting oneself to a razorblade and blunt saw together with two or three ancient chisels will inevitably produce something of inferior quality.

The range of tools needed to build any of the projects in this book is quite modest, and the list below contains all that is required. You will probably have most of them already, but they can all be purchased easily and cheaply.

Tenon Saw Most thicknesses of plywood up to ¼″ can be cut with a good quality sharp tenon saw. The large panels in even the biggest models – baseboard, side and rear walls and roof panels – are unlikely to exceed this width, and where I have referred to the use of ½″ plywood, this will only be for the baseboard and can be cut with power tools, or the supplier will cut it to size for you.

Fretsaw A fretsaw and set of assorted blades, available at a reasonable price from hobby shops and DIY stores, is the other essential saw. Fretsaws are easy to use with a little practice and are used to cut out door and window frames, fireplaces etc.

Cross-cut Saw This is the best tool for cutting polystyrene foam sheet.

Lino or Stanley Knife A lino or Stanley knife is an absolutely essential tool for modelling, and can be used on both foam and plywood. The Stanley knife can be fitted with different blades, increasing its usefulness – an Exacto tool set, which also offers various types of replaceable blades, is a versatile alternative.

Hammer You will need a small carpenter's hammer, especially when constructing a plywood house, to hammer in the numerous panel pins and decorative tiny nails. A **Punch** is also necessary for driving the panel pins below the surface of the wood.

Small Drill A small drill will be used mainly for making holes for screws and nails when hinging and for drilling into walls and beams to fit electric cables and wires. A hand or bobbin drill is acceptable, but an electric drill is ideal – a good selection of bits is essential for either.

Screwdrivers Apart from their obvious uses, a couple of small flat-headed screwdrivers will be helpful when decorating.

Eyebrow Tweezers will come in handy for picking up and positioning the small screws used in modelling.

Pliers It is best to have one flat and one pointed pair for cutting wire and panel pins, bending wire and other such uses.

Scissors are useful for cutting card and cardboard for roofing and decoration, and cutting thin metal sheets such as litho plate or thin aluminium.

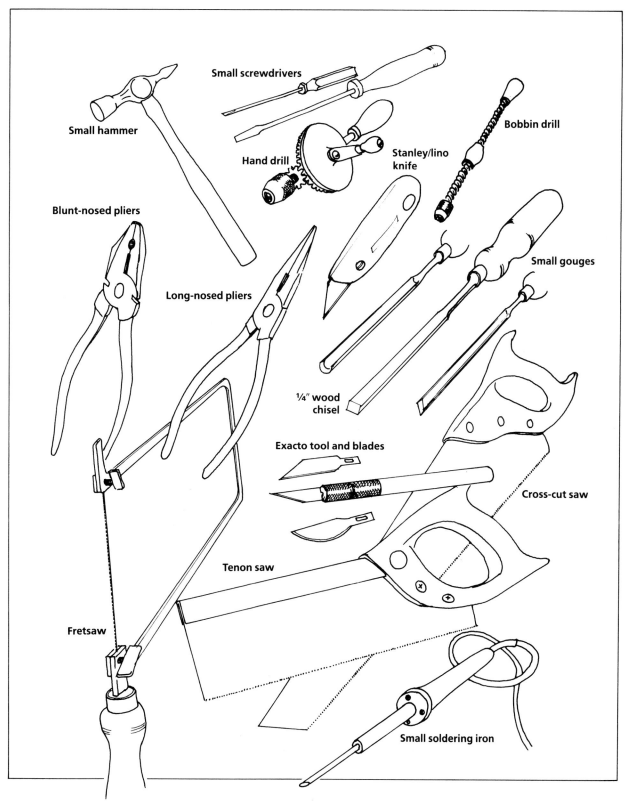

Small screwdrivers

Small hammer

Hand drill

Stanley/lino knife

Bobbin drill

Blunt-nosed pliers

Long-nosed pliers

Small gouges

¼" wood chisel

Exacto tool and blades

Cross-cut saw

Tenon saw

Fretsaw

Small soldering iron

Soldering Iron If you intend lighting your model, a soldering iron is essential. The electric ones are best for the purpose.

Rulers and Set Squares are essential in all stages of modelling, from checking the straightness of the walls to the final decoration.

Wood Chisel This is not an essential tool, but a ¼″ wood chisel will come in handy for marking out bricks in solid wood chimneys.

Sandpaper A pack of various grades is necessary.

Paintbrushes It is worth getting a good assortment, from the very small artists' sizes to about 1″ wide.

Gouges A set of small gouges will come in use to groove the floorboards and create decorative effects, as well as grooving ceilings and walls to take electric wiring.

. . . .

Although the list above contains all the essential tools to construct the houses and rooms, the process can be speeded up by the use of more sophisticated – and more expensive – tools.

The initial cost of buying a bandsaw – up to about £150 – may seem great, but this will be quickly offset by the many uses for the tool, not only in modelling but also in other types of woodwork. It is an endlessly versatile tool, and makes the cutting of wood for panelling not only easier but a good deal cheaper than purchasing stripwood from DIY or model shops.

The bandsaw can cut almost any dimension, as the only limit is the throat width – from the blade to the fence – and will take wood up to 3″ thick, which can come in very useful if you intend to use old wood. There is a great deal of satisfaction to be got from recycling well-seasoned old wood – old furniture, often given or even thrown away, is an excellent source.

It is worth considering buying an electric fretsaw, as this can simplify work as well as reducing the time spent on cutting. Apart from being necessary for working on the house, it can be used for making miniature furniture and fittings.

Small electric drill sets are not expensive to buy from most model shops – the ones that come with twist bits, buffers, engravers and perhaps a small circular saw attachment are the best investments. They are also useful in engraving and other hobbies and crafts.

CHAPTER FOUR

METHODS
AND MATERIALS

ALTERNATIVES TO PLYWOOD

Plywood is the commonest material used in building model houses, and is *essential* in all our models for the baseboards and front openings, which cannot be hinged if any other material is used. We also use plywood in our larger models – the country houses and 'hall' houses – but it is by no means the only construction material.

The best alternative is 1″ thick polystyrene insulating foam (though it comes in other sizes and thicknesses) – it is inexpensive and easily obtainable from building suppliers and some DIY stores. Even a large model house can be built from only three panels of 48″ × 20″ foam – this is for all exterior and interior walls and excludes the plywood floors, baseboard and front opening – and means a real saving over an all-wood construction.

This material is long-lasting, very strong and easy to work, requiring only a lino or Stanley knife or Exacto tool to cut – particularly useful when it

FIG 4.1 *Town house made from a variety of materials*

FIG 4.2 *Basic room*

comes to cutting out window and door frames, fireplaces etc.

There are other types and densities of foam, though these are less easily available than the soft white insulating foam. The hardest and densest is 'blue foam', used for boats, surfboards and model aircraft construction. This is harder to work than the insulating foam, and is also more expensive – consult the local Yellow Pages for manufacturers if you decide you want to use it.

Thick and fairly rigid cardboard, such as that used to pack large domestic appliances, is another easily found building material and by far the cheapest, as it is often discarded behind electrical and household goods shops. You can use both the solid and the corrugated types – the main use is for the roof of the house, but *only if it is not to be hinged or opened*. That said, it is extremely strong when supported and tiled, and can save on building a plywood roof.

GLAZING MATERIALS

Clear Perspex vinyl sheet or a similar plastic sheet, usually $^3/_{16}''$ thick, is the most common material to use for windows. It is available, often at off-cut prices, from your local DIY shop – don't be afraid to haggle over the price, as some shops will sometimes charge by the square foot even when the piece you require is only a long thin strip.

Perspex has one great advantage over the alternative, thick celluloid sheet, for the Georgian house modeller – it is possible to create bull's-eyes on Perspex or plastic, as shown in Chapter 7. This cannot be achieved on the thinner celluloid, which is also reasonably expensive. The advantages of using celluloid sheet are that it can be cut with scissors and can be very flexible even when framed, making it useful for curved or bay windows. This flexibility, however, makes it difficult to clean, and it is easily marked.

Of course the most authentic windows in a model will be made from glass, but this too has various disadvantages:

▌It is not at all easy to cut unless you are confident and experienced in using a glass cutter
▌The edges remain sharp when cut, so great care has to be taken in handling and fitting
▌It is easily broken, and should therefore not be used if children are going to play with the model
▌It is much heavier than clear plastics or celluloid.

On the plus side, it is easy to clean and almost impossible to scratch under normal conditions – weigh up these considerations carefully before committing yourself to using glass in your model.

METALS

The ideal metal to use for door hinges, gutterings, door plates and other small fixtures is litho plate, the best source of which is a printer who still uses the litho method – try the printers in your area. A good but expensive alternative is thin aluminium sheet about 22 swg thick, which can be purchased from model or craft shops. To save money, it is possible to straighten out beer or soft drink cans and use the metal, and yet another option is to use thin tin sheet. For hinges, brass strips or thin brass sheet can be bought in various thicknesses and widths from your local model shop.

GLUES

Most of the joints in a model house can be glued together with a good PVA wood glue, either white wood glue or clear wood glue – both appear white until dry. *Do not use any other types of glue on polystyrene foam as they can melt it!*

Impact adhesives, though messy to use, can be useful, and instant glue is handy for small jobs – it can, however, mark Perspex if used without due care, and must not be used on foam. *Do not use balsa cement anywhere near polystyrene as it will melt it very quickly.*

ROOFING MATERIALS

There is quite a good choice of materials to use for making a slate or tiled roof – black emery paper will produce a very authentic slate roof, but beware of running your fingers lovingly down it!

Another good slate finish can be achieved with black or very dark grey card, sold by art shops and office suppliers. Make sure that the colour goes all the way through, and choose card with a very hard surface texture as it is difficult to finish one with a porous surface.

For tiles, thick black paper gives a good appearance and is cheap and easy to use. It needs finishing with a matt varnish, however, and you will need to be careful about sticking it down thoroughly.

FIG 4.3 *Rooms in a small house*

The majority of ready-made (toy) dolls' houses are finished with painted or papered roofs, and in some cases the tiles are simply marked out on the roof – even relatively well-made and sophisticated houses have been finished in this manner. Of course the final choice rests with you, the builder, but we would be disappointed if our designs were to be finished in this way.

Individual tiles in slate or stone are available from specialist suppliers, as are ready-made stone, brick and ceramic chimney stacks and the like, but these are not only very expensive but also heavy – putting on individual tiles also takes quite a time.

Most miniatures shops stock wooden shingles ready cut – we do not feel that they are right for an English house, being appropriate to New England rather than the old country, but they can be painted for use as a Medieval stone roof. And, although this does not fall into the period covered by this book, it is worth mentioning that the most effective and acceptable material we know for a thatched roof is fine raffia, although innovative modellers may find other solutions.

ELECTRIC LIGHTING

Many electric lighting systems are currently available from specialist suppliers and magazines, and the modeller can consult them if expense is no object. Chapter 11 suggests some straightforward and inexpensive, though not inferior, alternatives and describes a simple method of lighting which can be adapted for as many rooms and fireplaces as required.

Until well into the Victorian era, houses would have been lit by candles or oil lamps, and, as far as we know, this cannot be done in a model house! So you must decide just to what degree of authenticity and scale fidelity you wish to go – this is true not only of the Georgian period, but also of any preceding ones.

Apart from deciding not to light the house at all – a waste of a lot of work and no way to show off

the fittings and furnishings, in our opinion – there are ways of producing quite authentic-looking illumination. The warm glow of a coal or wood fire can be produced by ready-made fire kits or can be produced by the modeller and lit electrically, and it is not difficult to make lanterns using electric bulbs, that look very like authentic oil lanterns. Wall sconces and candle-style bulbs – particularly those from Christmas tree sets – can also look excellent.

It is thus possible to stick to the furnishings and fittings of the period in your house by attention to the ways of lighting described in the relevant chapter. You can, however, make your period house one that has been adapted for living in later eras, for instance the Victorian age or even up to the present day. This will allow you to fit modern-style electric lighting and appliances.

FINISHING MATERIALS

Wooden floorboards and plain panelled walls will need a polished finish, particularly if they have been stained to the right colour. A modern-type high gloss would not appear correct for the period, and a smooth satin finish gives the aged look. Clear model aircraft dope is available from model shops and has many advantages. It can be applied with a paintbrush, it can be thinned with cellulose thinners (available from car accessory shops), and it also dries very quickly.

The first coat of two parts dope to one part thinner will dry in about 15 minutes, and when dry should be lightly sanded with fine sandpaper before another coat is applied. One further sanding with the finest grade of paper and a wax polishing will bring floorboards up to a fine standard, although two coats are sufficient (without the second sanding).

Wood panelling should have a higher gloss, so we recommend two coats of thinned dope and one coat of unthinned dope, with the sanding between coats and the final polishing the same as for the floorboards.

FIG 4.4 *Elaborate fireplace and contrasting panelling*

The quick-drying qualities of dope mean that you have to work fast with it, but this is an advantage rather than the reverse. Many varnish wood finishes are available, but they take much longer to dry than dope, and most require the use of a wood filler first, which both costs more and takes up more time.

Another finish that requires little drying time is 'button polish', used in French polishing and available from DIY shops. Like dope, it must be worked quickly if applied with a brush, but this process can be slowed down by the addition of a few drops of linseed oil. Again, sand this finish down between coats. Having tried most of the wood finishes on the market, we find dope the best for speed and convenience, with button polish nearly as good.

Emulsion paints, which come in a huge variety of colours and tints, are excellent for both interior and exterior finishing. The paint dries quite quickly and, as it is water-based, brushes can be easily cleaned so additional coats can be applied without much delay, though these coats may not always be necessary. Textured emulsion paint is also available, and this can be useful for wall and ceiling finishing. If you decide to use oil-based paints, remember to apply undercoat to the bare wood first.

Guttering and downspouts are rarely finished in high gloss, and the best paint to use on these is matt black, which is either oil- or water-based, the latter drying very quickly.

You will need plaster for many interior and exterior jobs on your model house – we use Tetrion filler, available from DIY shops. Compared with wall or ceiling plasters, it is quite slow-setting, though this can work to your advantage, and a little will go a long way, even if it is relatively expensive.

Fibreglass resin is also useful, particularly when making illuminated or 'glow' fireplaces. *Do not use this material in direct contact with foam as it will melt it.* The resin is available from car accessory shops, and, again, a little goes a long way.

CHAPTER FIVE

FLOORS

*I*N EARLY GEORGIAN HOUSES random-sized planks were utilised for floorboards, but in the later Georgian and Regency periods (particularly in expensive town houses) floors would almost invariably be built with boards symmetrically cut out of hardwood. Marble in contrasting colours was quite often used in kitchens and halls, and the early Georgian builders still made great use of stone flags in country houses. These would also be used in kitchens and hallways, and would in the main be symmetrical rather than random.

There were, however, no hard and fast rules – building methods were usually dictated by area and by the affluence of the person who commissioned the building – and this means that there is a wide choice of floorings available to the model builder. Methods of construction for all these floors are included in this chapter.

Considerable thought must be given to the choice of floor finishings, and time and effort must be expended to get the best results. Commercially-produced floor planking can be purchased and the results can be very pleasing, as the photographs of the ground floor of the shop and the single box room show. These floorings are obviously more expensive than those made by the builder, but much time can be saved. The flooring used in the examples mentioned above comes ready laid on a sheet and only requires cutting to size and gluing down after staining and polishing. Stone and marble floorings are also available ready-made, and the addresses of the manufacturers and stockists are given at the end of the book.

FIG 5.1 *Wooden floor*

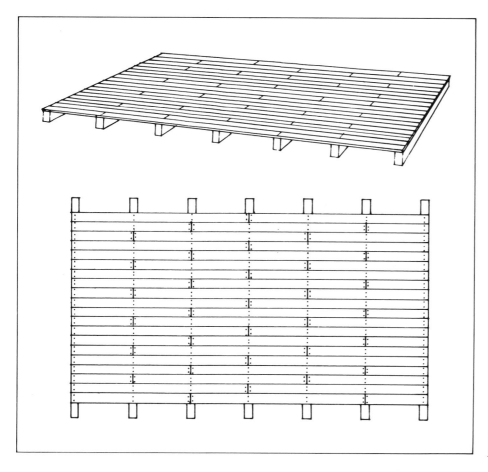

FIG 5.2 *Wooden floor marked out on plywood*

FIG 5.3 *Position of plank joins and nail markings*

WOODEN FLOORS

The most authentic method of making a wooden floor is to lay each single plank over the roof beams – this, however satisfying, is time-consuming, involves much forward planning for such essentials as chimney breasts and stairwells, and should really only be attempted by the experienced builder. Instructions for this method are given later in this section – for the relative beginner or inexperienced modeller, a plywood floor is simple to make and can be very effective if done properly.

The first and most important thing to remember about wooden floorboarding, whether simulated or laid plank by plank, is that *it should always run at right angles to the roof beams*, even if these are not visible – lack of attention to such detail may not concern the casual observer, but an expert would

notice. So it is worth deciding beforehand which way the roof beams would run in your model.

Refer to Fig 5.2 for a method of marking floorboards that closely approximates the original. Choose a straight-grained piece of ⅛″ plywood – softwood will be easier to mark – and mark out the floorboards as shown with a hard carpenter's pencil.

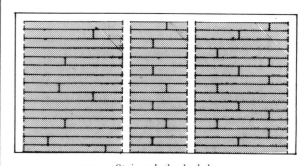

FIG 5.4 *Stain only the shaded areas*

FIG 5.5 *Finished wooden floor*

You will need to press quite hard to leave a mark, and will have to go over each line two or three times. Alternatively, grooving the wood with a small gouge along the side of a ruler is equally effective, and you will not have to exert as much pressure. Remember to mark the floor in the opposite direction from the roof beams.

Mark where the planks join, as shown in Fig 5.3, using a hard ordinary pencil, and also mark the nail positions along the line of the roof beams. As can be seen, the nails are in pairs on either side of the plank joins.

Another method for marking the nails is to use a 2″ round nail – tap this gently with a hammer to produce the nail marks. This marking can be tedious, but is the best way to create an authentic impression.

The floor is now ready to be stained – it is vital to mark out the areas which must be left free of stain and other finishes. These are the parts where you will later glue the side, rear and internal walls, and is particularly important in houses where foam walls are used, as they are always glued on to the baseboard – *see* Fig 5.4. (In houses with plywood walls, the stain can be taken to the edges of the floor, as the rear and side walls are panel-pinned to the sides of the floor.)

For Georgian house floors, the best shades of stain are Mid-Oak, Walnut and Dark Oak. Make sure you use a spirit stain, as water-based stains could warp the floor. When the stain has dried, finish the floor in clear model aircraft dope or French polish, as described in Chapter 3.

The method mentioned above, of laying individual floorboards directly on to the plywood base, is illustrated in Fig 5.6. The floorboards should be

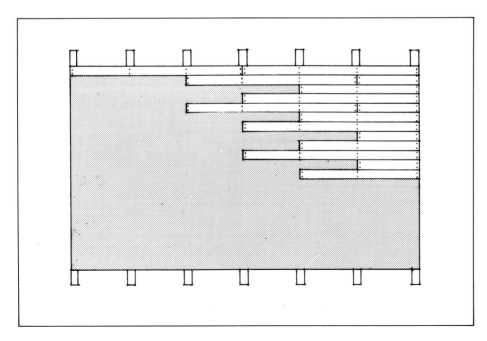

FIG 5.6 *Nailing on individual floorboards*

FIG 5.7 *Basic marble floor*

½″ × ⅛″ and can be cut from stripwood of almost any kind, available from model shops and some DIY shops. Glue the boards into position, ensuring that they join over a beam, and then nail them at the appropriate places using tiny ¼″ black nails, available from specialist miniature shops. To do this accurately will take a long time and will be expensive, as you will need literally hundreds of nails, but the excellent authentic result makes it all worth your while. Stain and finish the floor as described above and in Chapter 3.

MARBLE FLOORS

The contrasting black and white marble squares used for many Georgian halls and kitchens are best made out of Formica off-cuts. These can be available very cheaply from DIY shops, and the only possible disadvantage is that they are difficult to cut satisfactorily – a fretsaw or bandsaw will give the best results. The squares should be cut approximately 1″ square and glued down in a chequered pattern – *see* Fig 5.7.

Small squares of Fablon (also available from DIY shops) can also be used, and ready-made squares can be obtained from specialist suppliers, but these can prove expensive.

STONE FLOORS

There are two main methods of reproducing stone floors – the first is to use dark or slate grey stone paint. Paint two or three coats – enough to prevent the wood grain of the baseboard from showing through – on to the baseboard, sanding between applications. When dry, use a fine brush and a slightly darker or a slightly lighter paint to mark out slabs into approximately 2″ squares – some cracks and irregularities can be incorporated for a good effect. Finish with a coat of matt varnish.

The second and most authentic method is to use a real roof slate. Building suppliers will be able to supply and cut slates to the exact measurements at little expense – unless you have experience at cutting roof slates, it is best to get the supplier to do this, as it is all too easy to ruin a slate.

FIG 5.8 *Marble kitchen floor*

When you have a correctly sized slate, mark it out with a 'scribe', or a 6″ nail with a sharp point – one design for marking is shown in Fig 5.9. Take care that the scribe or nail does not slip and leave unwanted marks.

To finish your slate, first wipe it all over with methylated spirit, which will not only clean and prepare the underside to receive glue, but also clean off any discolouration or chalkiness. While it is drying completely, make a pad from cotton wool wrapped in a piece of cotton material fixed to a small handle, illustrated in Fig 5.10. You will also need French polish and linseed oil, both available from art or DIY shops – dip the pad into the linseed oil and then the French polish and apply it to the cleaned slate, rubbing in well with a circular motion.

Keep the pad moving, as French polish dries quickly – if the pad begins to feel sticky, dip it occasionally into the linseed oil. When you have completely covered the slate, let it dry for a few minutes before giving it another coat – three or four should be enough, by which time the slate will have the slight sheen normally only achieved by

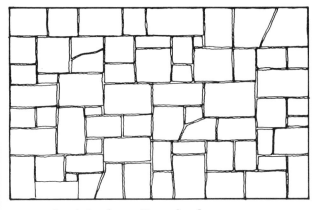

FIG 5.9 *One design for marking a slate floor*

many generations of wear and tear. Allow the slate to fully dry and then glue it on to the plywood baseboard.

It is possible to buy ready-made slates from the suppliers and stockists listed at the back of the book, but these can be heavy and costly.

FIG 5.10 *Cotton and cotton wool pad*

CHAPTER SIX

DOORS

————

M AKING DOORS FOR ALMOST any period house is relatively simple but requires, as in all modelling, care and attention to detail. Illustrated in this chapter are all the types of door used in the Georgian and Regency eras. The comparatively plain board doors would have been suitable for outbuildings, kitchens and servants' quarters, while the doors shown in Fig 6.2 are more representative of interior doors. Double doors were widely used in larger houses.

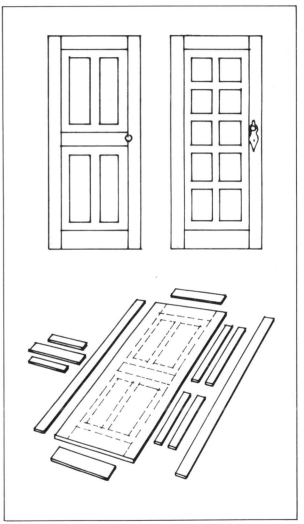

FIG 6.2 *Interior doors and exploded view of four-panelled door*

FIG 6.1 *Front door in dressed stone setting*

All the doors featured in the country house were produced from the methods shown in this chapter, while extensive use of ready-made doors can be seen in the other houses – see the list of suppliers and stockists of doors at the back of the book.

Doorknobs can also be purchased from these suppliers, but an alternative is to use brass or copper upholstery studs glued on to the door.

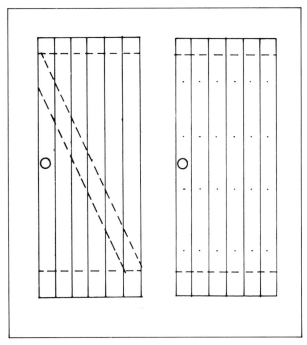

FIG 6.3 *Simple doors with planking marked*

SIMPLE DOORS

The plain doors shown in Fig 6.3 can be cut from ¼″ thick plywood, whitewood or hardwood – if you have used wooden walls, then it is possible to use the piece cut out for the doorway to make the door. As for floors, there are two ways to mark the planking detail. The first is to press down hard with a carpenter's pencil along a ruler – if this is done two or three times, it will leave a small indentation in the wood and a dark line which, when stained and covered by varnish, dope or French polish, will look realistic. The other method is to mark the wood with a gouge (as illustrated in Fig 6.4) or lino knife, to a depth of no more than ¹⁄₁₆″ on both sides.

The crossbars should be no more than ⅛″ thick and around ¼″ or ⅜″ wide and made from balsa wood or very thin softwood, available from model and miniaturist shops. Glue the crossbars into position. For a different effect, the diagonal crossbar can be left off and you can create a nailed effect on both sides by either using brass or black miniature nails or by marking with a black felt-tip pen before varnishing.

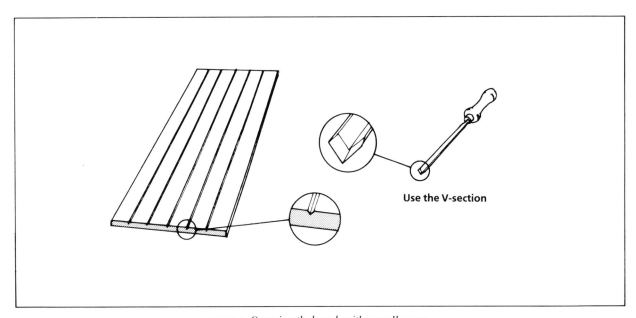

Use the V-section

FIG 6.4 *Grooving the boards with a small gouge*

28

HINGES

Ready-made hinges are available from a number of miniature manufacturers, and come in a variety of sizes and styles. Fitting them is a tricky procedure as, being miniature versions of full-size hinges, the door and frame must be recessed as shown in Fig 6.6, and they must be attached with very small pins. They are also difficult to install, so accuracy in positioning them is essential.

Many doors of the early Georgian period were strap hinged – look at Fig 6.7 for an illustration of this method. Strip the heads off nails and bend them

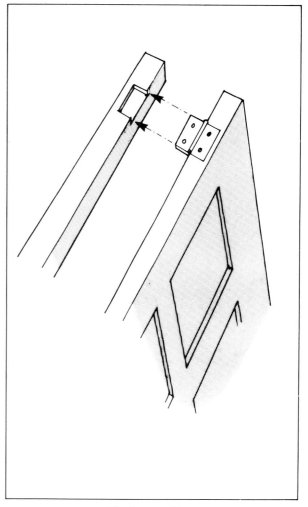

FIG 6.6 *The frame and door must be recessed for miniature hinges*

FIG 6.5 *Six-panelled door in dressed stone setting*

at right angles before pushing them into the frame with pliers. This will create a peg on to which to drop the strap hinges themselves, which are cut to the shape shown from litho plate, strip aluminium or thin brass or copper strip, and are then bent round a nail larger than the one used for the peg. You can measure the hinges by laying the wall flat and putting the door in place then judging how big the hinge should be.

Fig 6.9 shows another method of hinging, using Mylar strip – again lay the wall flat and place the door in the doorway. Glue two pieces of Mylar strip

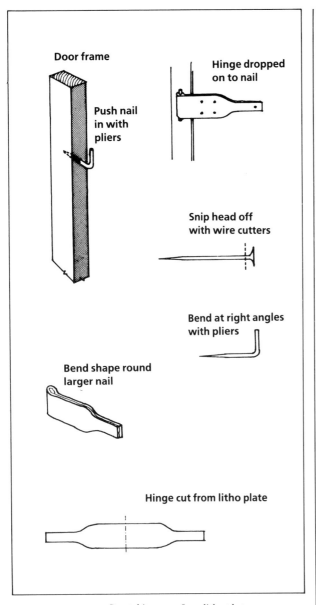

Door frame

Push nail in with pliers

Hinge dropped on to nail

Snip head off with wire cutters

Bend at right angles with pliers

Bend shape round larger nail

Hinge cut from litho plate

FIG 6.7 *Strap hinge cut from litho plate*

¼″–½″ wide to the door and frame as shown using instant glue. A plain or moulded frame can then be glued into place, and this door framing will hide the Mylar strip on the door, assuming that you wish to hide the hinging.

Another method of hinging, featured in many ready-made doors and furniture, is shown in Fig 6.10. It is used more for exterior than interior doors, and requires a crosspiece across the floor, but is otherwise quite acceptable. You will have to make up the frame and crosspiece before fitting them in to the wall.

As can be seen in the illustration, the edge of the door that is to take the hinging must be rounded off for easy opening and closing before a nail hole is drilled top and bottom. Thin panel pins are then nailed through the top of the frame and the underside of the crosspiece into the pre-drilled holes. The entire frame, door and crosspiece are then fitted into the wall.

FIG 6.8 *Door with two steps and dressed stone and brick setting*

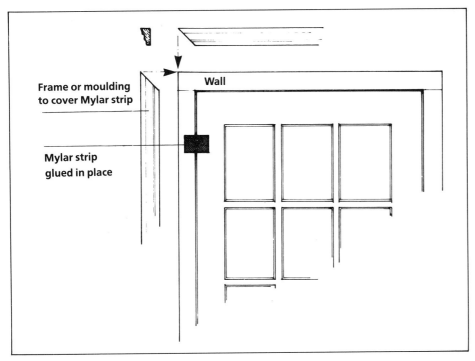

FIG 6.9 *Hinge using Mylar strip*

Frame or moulding
to cover Mylar strip

Wall

Mylar strip
glued in place

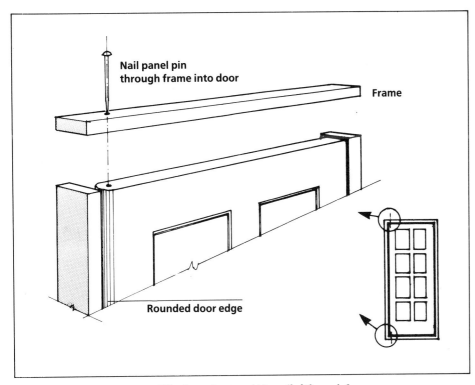

Nail panel pin
through frame into door

Frame

Rounded door edge

FIG 6.10 *Hinging using panel pin nailed through frame*

FIG 6.11 *Three types of multi-pane glass door*

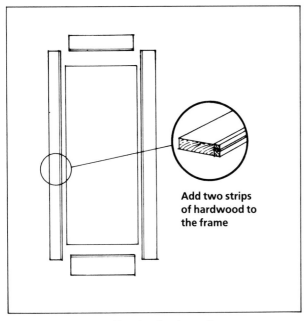

FIG 6.12 *Framing for glass or Perspex*

GLASS PANE DOORS

Fig 6.11 shows examples of three types of multi-pane glass door – these can easily be made from ready-made grooved stripwood, or you can make your own up. Using the ready-made frame, cut three sides to size and make them up before adding the clear plastic panes and finishing by gluing in the remaining side – *see* Fig 6.12. If you wish to make your own frames, refer to the detail in the illustration and add two strips of $1/16''$ balsa wood or

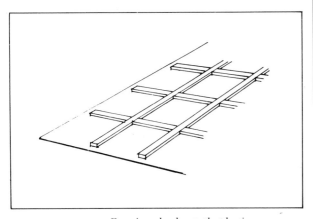

FIG 6.13 *Framing glued on to the plastic*

FIG 6.14 *Brick setting for town house door*

hardwood to each frame edge, leaving a gap in the middle for the plastic.

The framing for the panes is made in the same way as for window panes – *see* Fig 6.13 – $1/16''$ beech or balsa can be bought from model shops, and can be glued on to the plastic with UHU or a similar glue. Remember to paint the framing before adding it to the plastic. Also refer to Chapter 7 for how to bull's-eye the glass panes for an authentic finish.

OTHER DOORS

The doors described above are very authentic, but if you wish to construct a door exactly as you would a full-size one, this is possible. You will need six lengths of wood ½″ × 6″ × approximately ¼″ – lay these in place as shown in Fig 6.3, and glue them together as closely as possible. Frame the top and bottom with ⅛″ softwood or balsa wood and add a diagonal as shown. As with the plain doors, you can either put in small nails or mark with a black felt-tip pen before staining and finishing.

DOUBLE DOORS

Double doors are ideal for a large model incorporating a grand hall or even a very large room – they give a good feeling of scale and can be either wooden or glass pane doors (16 panes were often used in each door). Make the two basic halves of the door as for glass or wooden doors and hinge them in your chosen style. Double doors must always have a stop made – this can easily be made by extending the framing either on the front or rear of the wall by ¹⁄₁₆″ (*see* Fig 6.15), and in some cases a stop down each side may be advisable.

These doors can jam together quite easily, so make sure there is a small gap between them – this can be covered with a wooden facing as shown in Fig 6.16, or by carefully rebating the doors. This is by far the neatest option, but you will need rebating tools to achieve it – one alternative is to glue on a strip of wood half the thickness of the door to each door, as shown in Fig 6.16.

FIG 6.15 *Door stop for double doors*

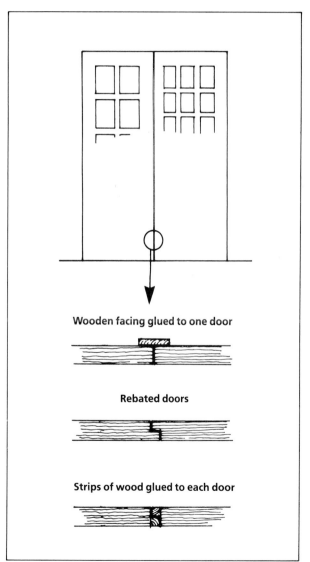

Wooden facing glued to one door

Rebated doors

Strips of wood glued to each door

FIG 6.16 *Three methods of covering a gap*

FRAMES

Ready-made door and window framing and architrave can be obtained from several miniature
manufacturers, and a few examples of a wide range
of mouldings are illustrated in Fig 6.17. It is, of
course, possible to make your own mouldings if
you possess a router, but this is a rather expensive
piece of machinery and the use of it requires skill.
If a lot of model houses are to be built, it may
prove to be a worthwhile investment (the same is
true of many power tools), otherwise the cost may
be prohibitive.

It is possible to produce a simple but effective
door framing and architrave using a reasonably
soft woodstrip – beech, hard balsa, whitewood –
about $\frac{3}{8}'' \times \frac{1}{8}''$. Cut this to the required length and
sand or plane one side to the rounded shape shown
in Fig 6.19. To give a moulded appearance, groove
along each length with a hard pencil along a ruler,
pressing deeply. If done properly, a fairly deep
groove can be obtained, and the pencil marks will
not show when painted.

Skirting boards can also be made in this manner,
and the results of a single groove board so achieved
can be seen in photographs of the country house.
As always, experiment until the best results are
obtained.

FIG 6.18 *Country house door and porch*

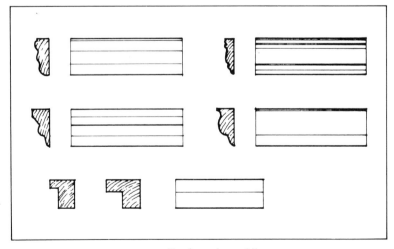

FIG 6.17 *Ready-made mouldings*

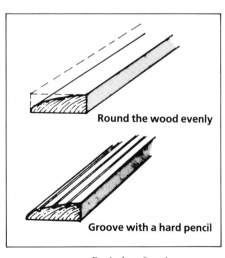

Round the wood evenly

Groove with a hard pencil

FIG 6.19 *Basic door framing*

CHAPTER SEVEN

WINDOWS

*T*HE BUILDER OF Georgian and Regency house models has the choice of producing windows for him or herself by the methods shown in this chapter or purchasing ready-made or kit form windows from the wide range available from the specialist suppliers and stockists listed at the end of the book.

FIG 7.1 *Dormer and sash multi-pane windows*

It is not difficult to make fixed windows with a good scale appearance, and attention to the drawings in this chapter will pay dividends. Sash, i.e. opening, windows can also be made – the country house model shows both types. Early Georgian house window panels would often have dimpled or bull's-eye glass in some of the panels, and there is a method of reproducing this.

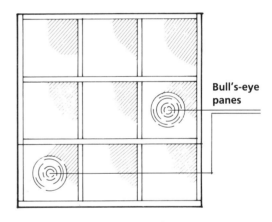

Bull's-eye panes

FIG 7.2 *Nine-paned window*

FIXED WINDOWS

Fig 7.2 shows a simple nine-paned window which can be constructed directly on to the wall of your model. Cut out the opening to the desired size and, using stripwood (obtainable from most model shops in a variety of hardwoods), frame the interior surround from the back with $\frac{1}{2}'' \times \frac{1}{16}''$ strip, as shown by the detail in Fig 7.3.

Next cut a piece of Perspex or similar clear rigid strip to the correct size to fit snugly into the window opening, and glue it neatly into place using UHU, impact adhesive or similar glue sparingly round the edges.

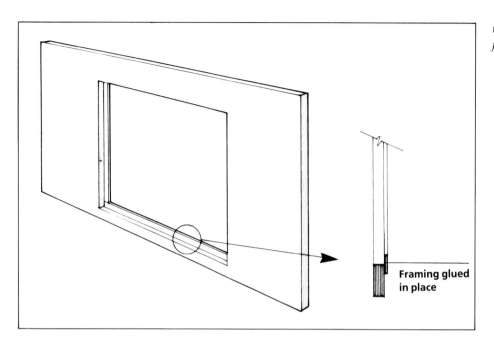

FIG 7.3 *Framing window from the back*

Framing glued in place

FIG 7.4 *12-paned window*

As most of the wood used in the construction of your model will rarely be thicker than ¼″ and your clear sheet will be between ³⁄₃₂″ and ⅛″, you must select your panel framing from a strip that takes these widths into consideration (do not overlook the possibility of using real picture glass if you are an experienced glass cutter). For instance, if the wall thickness is ¼″ and the Perspex is ⅛″, then ⅛″ square section stripwood would be ideal, whereas if the wall is only ⅛″ thick, then the thickness of the framing strip would depend upon the thickness of the Perspex.

Paint the wood before starting the panel divisions – my daughter and I always do this, and we prefer to use quick-drying sprays available from car accessory shops or DIY stores. You will require two cans, one of undercoat and one of gloss. When the wood is perfectly dry and the glass has been marked out in appropriately sized squares – this is best done with a ballpoint pen, as the marks are easy to wipe off – cut the framing to the right size and glue it into place with UHU or a similar adhesive. Ordinary butt joints are all that is needed, but you can also make slotted joints as shown in Fig 7.5.

FIG 7.5 *Slotted joints*

FIG 7.6 *Two methods of framing a window*

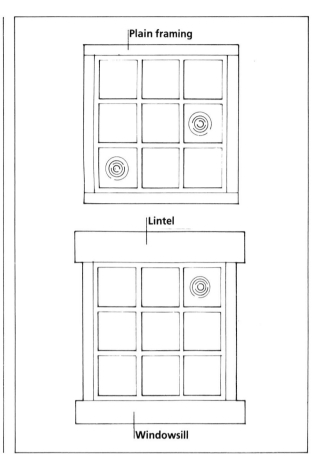

Again, it is usually only necessary to glue the framing to the front of the Perspex, but there is no reason why you should not frame the back as well.

The outside frame of the window can now be added – plain framing may be applied all round or a piece representing a lintel (approximately ¾″ × ¹⁄₁₆″) can be added to the top of the window. Side frames should be, say, ¹⁄₁₆″ × ¼″, and finally a piece ½″ square can be used for the windowsill – Fig 7.6 shows both types of framing.

The same method can be used to make variations, and three examples are shown in Fig 7.7 – the window on the left features 18 panes and a rounded top to the frame. A fancy architrave may be used for the side framing if appropriate. The window on the right has side-opening casement-type windows, divided by two pieces of stripwood – see Chapter 6 for how to add these.

FIG 7.7 *Three styles of 18-paned windows*

FIG 7.8 *Show window for the shop*

OPENING WINDOWS

It is a little more complicated to make windows that open, but it can be very rewarding.

Either glue together $\frac{1}{4}'' \times \frac{1}{2}''$ or $\frac{1}{8}''$ square wood to form the shape shown in Fig 7.9, or use ready-made sectioned wood to make the basic frames for a pair of casement windows to fit your window opening, rounding off the corners that are to be hinged. Drill a small hole in the top and bottom of each casement frame and tap in a small peg, fixing it in place with a tiny round nail, and drill a corresponding hole in the top and bottom of the frames. Slot the casement pegs into the bottom holes in the frames, and drop the top piece of the frame on to the top pegs, gluing the join at the corner. Fig 7.10 shows how it all fits together. Glue the casements in the frame into the opening and leave to dry.

BULL'S-EYE WINDOWS

My method of making a bull's-eye pane (there are likely to be two or more in a multi-pane window) is to heat an aluminium or metal knitting needle over a gas flame. The needle must be large, with the end at least $\frac{1}{2}''$ in diameter.

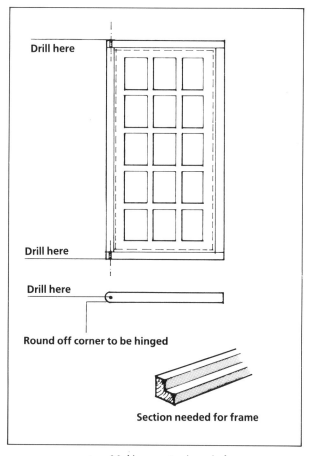

FIG 7.9 *Making an opening window*

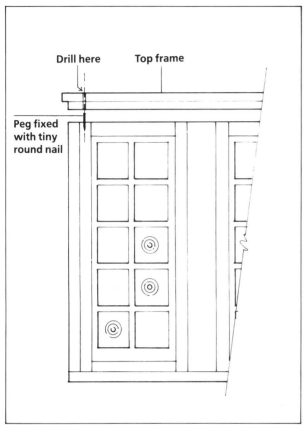

FIG 7.10 *Framing an opening window*

Having decided which panes you wish to bull's-eye, insulate the pointed end of the needle (the end you will hold) with insulating tape as shown, as heat travels quickly along the needle. The round end of the needle should now be placed over a low gas flame – *see* Fig 7.11 – *do not put the end directly over the flame*, as this could dirty it and ruin the process.

Experiment with a spare piece of glazing material until the right temperature is gained. The round end should be applied quite firmly to the chosen pane and then removed with a twisting motion – you will need practice, but the results can look very authentic, as seen in Figs 7.2, 7.6 and 7.7.

Windows and doors are modelling projects in themselves, and care and attention in their construction is more than worthwhile. Care in painting is absolutely essential, as sloppily painted windows will spoil the appearance of any model, no matter how well constructed – poor painting will also inhibit the action of the sliding windows, making them impossible to open.

This, unfortunately, can also be a problem with casement windows – too much paint will make them jam either in the open position or in the closed position. You have been warned! As my father used to say, if a job's worth doing it's worth doing well.

FIG 7.12 *Opening sash windows and half basement windows*

FIG 7.11 *Heating a knitting needle for bull's-eye glass*

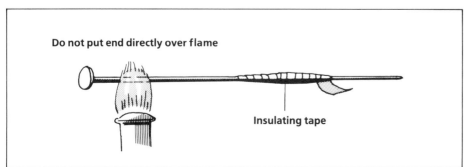

Do not put end directly over flame

Insulating tape

CHAPTER EIGHT

BEAMS AND PANELLING

BEAMING IN GEORGIAN HOUSES, particularly early ones, would have been largely restricted to kitchens, basement rooms and servants' quarters. Adze-marked beams would certainly still have been in evidence in small country houses, while in larger town and country houses they would have tended to be symmetrically cut and most likely planed to a smooth finish. They would often have been painted, sometimes in dark shades and sometimes to match the colour of the ceiling. The modeller must therefore know how to produce both smooth and marked types so that the appropriate beams can be put in the kind of house in which they are most likely to be found.

Similarly with wood panelling – once out of the Jacobean period, we find that extensive use was made of panelling on almost all kinds of Georgian buildings. With the extensive use of machinery that could cut wood in large symmetrical sections and to a wide range of thicknesses, wood panelling would quite often go from floor to ceiling, and would not depend on the horizontal and vertical

FIG 8.1 *Oak-style panelling in the country house*

strips used to cover the many joints in Medieval panelled rooms. Having said that, Jacobean-type panelling was used in many houses quite a long way into the Georgian period, particularly in country houses.

BEAMS

There are no standard thicknesses of beam for interior use, but observation of full-sized houses shows that the heavy master beams could be from 6″ to 12″ square. Assuming that your model house is ¹⁄₁₂ scale, this would make the beams ½″ to 1″ square, while in smaller houses ¼″ square or ¼″ × ³⁄₈″ would be used. We try to use oak where possible, but whitewood is also effective if well stained – experiment first – and very hard balsa wood can be used but is more difficult to stain convincingly.

Very few beams would have been of regular dimensions in older cottages and small houses – they would have been cut approximately, and this is what you should aim for if authenticity is desired. Beware, though – it is only too easy to overdo the random sizing, which can result in an over-stylised caricature, not a convincing model!

In Fig 8.2 the beams have been marked regularly with a lino knife or Exacto tool – the marks are on every ½″. Note that the beam should only be marked on the top two edges, as accurate gluing to

ceiling or wall can best be achieved with a flat surface. Although a better method than leaving all the edges square, this way can still look mass-produced or even 'stockbroker Georgian'.

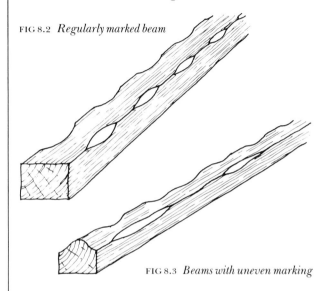

FIG 8.2 *Regularly marked beam*

FIG 8.3 *Beams with uneven marking*

My daughter and I use a second method – cut the timber to the required length and then slightly vary the width of the beam, as shown in Fig 8.3, cutting away as indicated with an Exacto tool or sharp lino knife. Now pare away the two top edges, again referring to the illustration and remembering to leave the underside square for effective and secure gluing.

FIG 8.4 *Unevenly marked beams in position*

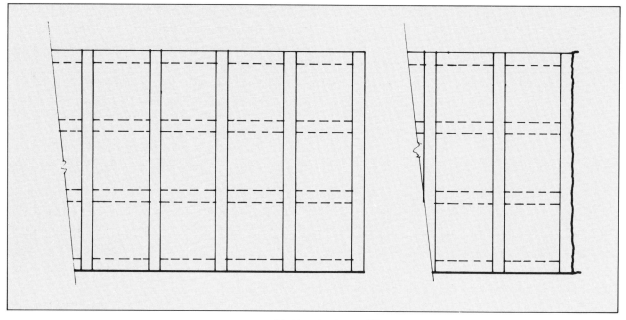

FIG 8.5 *Making simple panelling*

The photographs featuring beams in the part- and fully-completed models will reveal what you should aim for, and when stained to the right shade, each beam will be a work of art in itself. It can be a long and tedious business, but the end result is well worth it.

SIMPLE PANELLING

Wood panelling is a typical feature of the early Georgian house, and many thousands of fine examples may still be visited to provide inspiration for the modeller. If there are no such houses in your immediate area, check in your local library for books on the interiors of Georgian houses, which will also be an excellent source of information.

A simple wall of an early Georgian house is shown in Fig 8.5. As with all other decoration, this should be made before the model is assembled.

For a house with plywood walls, stain the plywood an appropriate colour and allow it to dry completely – my daughter and I use a very dark oak stain. You will need to cut at least 25 feet of wood for the panelling strips, which should then be stained to the same shade as the walls and allowed to dry.

Glue the dry vertical strips of wood to the panelling as shown in Fig 8.5, using PVA wood glue. (The vertical timber in the corner of the room should be slightly thicker to represent a corner post.) When they are completely dry, place the cross members – indicated in the diagram by dotted lines – into position between them. Perfect symmetry is not essential, although you will want to be accurate – perfection is often inappropriate to the period and can detract from the charm of your model.

For models built with polystyrene foam sheet walls, all that is necessary is to glue the finished panelling to the wall with wood or PVA glue – *do not use impact adhesive,* as this will attack and melt the foam.

GEORGIAN AND JACOBEAN STYLE PANELLING

The stripwood for a three-quarter-panelled Jacobean wall should be cut rather more precisely than that above, and should measure approximately $3/8'' \times 1/8''$. Mark the strip at $1\frac{1}{2}''$ intervals and cut away

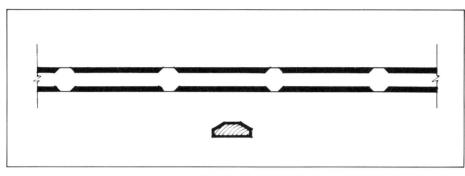

FIG 8.6 *Cutting the stripwood*

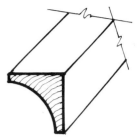

FIG 8.8 *Contour moulding for shelf*

the shaded part shown in Fig 8.6, using a lino knife or Exacto tool as before. Carve the profile shown.

After the vertical strips have been glued into place and are dry, cut and profile the cross members in the same way and glue them into position at each 1½″ interval as shown in Fig 8.7.

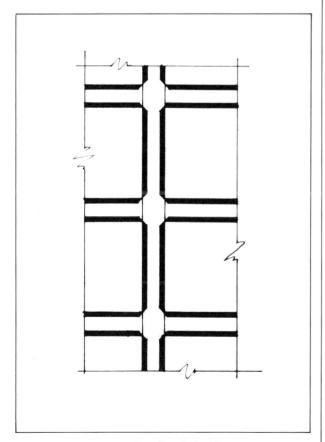

FIG 8.7 *Panelling in position*

DIY stores stock the contour moulding shown in Fig 8.8, which is ideal to support a narrow shelf above the wood-panelled wall – only a thin support is needed, so you will not require much contour moulding.

Cut off ⅛″ thick sections and stain them to the same colour as the panelling before gluing them in place. The shelf itself is made from a thin strip of wood also stained and glued on, and is a perfect place to display miniature plates and brassware. A completed Jacobean-style wall can be seen in Fig 8.9.

The fairly simple panelling used in the early Georgian period (and also in the country house – *see* photographs) is illustrated in Fig 8.11 and shows the large panels of wood referred to earlier. The panelling can be taken up to the ceiling, but is more often finished as shown, leaving a frieze. In this kind of panelling all the joints are mitred, so a mitre board is an essential piece of equipment.

In larger, more opulent houses, symmetrically sectioned framing would be used, with the additional architrave added after all the main framing had been completed. The use of a mitre board is again necessary, but only on the architrave, as shown in Fig 8.12.

Fig 8.13 shows how large wood panels were often decorated with architrave alone, without wide wood framings. As before, the panelling might reach the ceiling or might be finished to leave room for a frieze. The top of the architrave was often rounded,

FIG 8.9 *Completed Jacobean panelling*

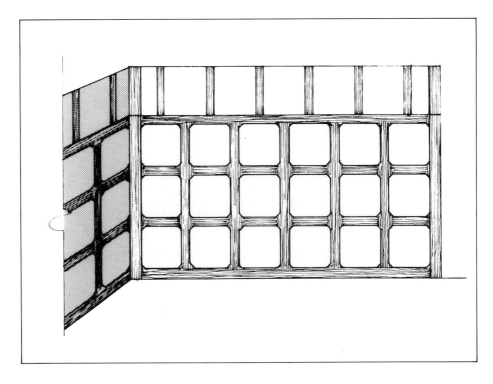

FIG 8.10 *Wooden panelling with double doors*

and sometimes, as in Fig 8.14, both top and bottom would be rounded.

Many exotic imported woods were employed in this panelling, and more often than not it would be finished solely by polishing to show the wood off to its best advantage. However, fashions change, and the original wood panelling might easily have been painted over in contrasting shades, with gilt used extensively on the architrave. The area inside the architrave would sometimes be filled with a hand-painted mural or hand-painted papers. Once again, I think the rule must be to observe and interpret – the choice available in the decoration of Georgian and Regency interiors would certainly appear endless – and great pleasure can be taken in the planning.

Finally, I should add that if the house construction is to be partly of polystyrene foam sheet, the walls must first be covered with thin plywood – $1/16''$ is sufficient. If all-paper decoration is to be used, this can be applied directly to the foam, as in the two-roomed Regency house.

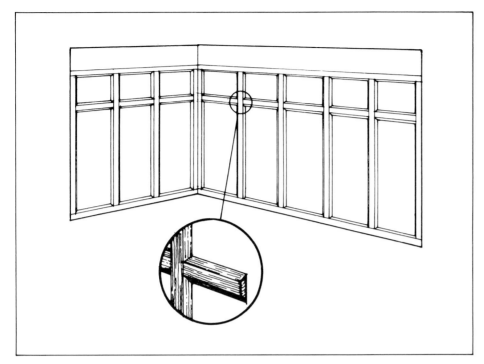

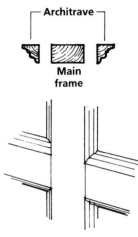

FIG 8.11 *Simple early Georgian panelling*

Architrave

Main frame

FIG 8.12 *Mitre and add the architrave*

FIG 8.13 *Large wood panels decorated with architrave*

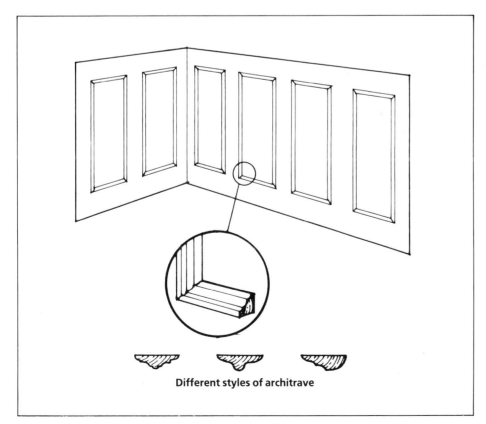

Different styles of architrave

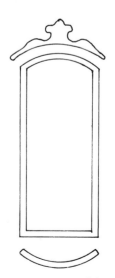

FIG 8.14 *A more elaborate rounded design*

FIREPLACES

IREPLACES ARE OFTEN TREATED as an afterthought in many models, especially if they are not the elegant decorated ones found in Georgian and Regency sitting rooms and lounges. But a fireplace is a focal point in any room, whether full-sized or miniature, and should be constructed and decorated with care and attention.

There is a wide range of fireplaces for Georgian houses available from the stockists and suppliers listed at the back of the book, and some of them are very good scale models. If, however, you either cannot run to the expense of a ready-made fireplace, or wish to create your own, this chapter provides details on building methods.

Whatever style you choose, all fireplaces require a hearth stone – an ordinary roof slate is ideal, but slates are difficult to cut to size, and a single floor tile in the appropriate colour can be purchased from DIY shops. Make sure you cut a large enough piece for the base and surround, as shown in the photographs in this book, and position it carefully and symmetrically.

FIG 9.1 *Simple domestic fireplace*

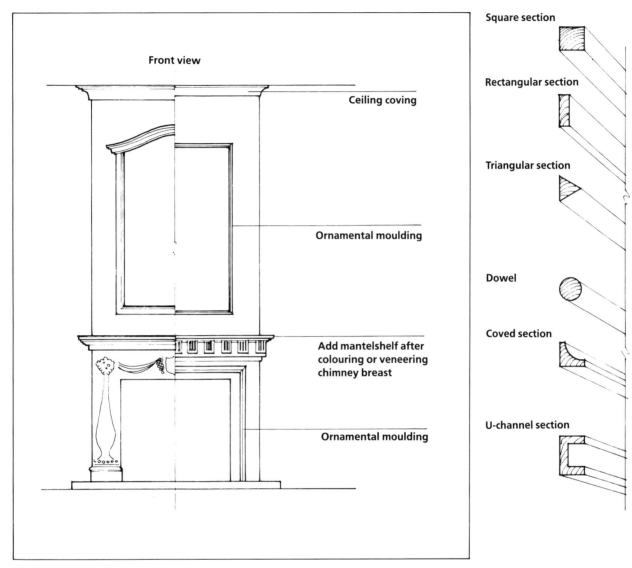

Front view

Ceiling coving

Ornamental moulding

Add mantelshelf after colouring or veneering chimney breast

Ornamental moulding

Square section

Rectangular section

Triangular section

Dowel

Coved section

U-channel section

FIG 9.2 *Two elegant fireplaces*

FIG 9.3 *Types of mouldings*

DECORATIVE FIREPLACES

Fig 9.2 shows two kinds of decoration for an elegant Georgian fireplace. In each case, there are alternative materials – 1″ whitewood, balsa wood or high-density foam – from which to make the chimney breast, and the surface is then veneered or painted before adding mouldings such as those illustrated in Fig 9.3 and 9.4. The photographs in this chapter show various designs used in the houses in this book.

Cut the fireplace opening with a fretsaw to the shape and size you require (the photographs should provide some ideas) – the wall of the model creates the fireback. Paint or veneer the chimney breast and decorate it with ornamental mouldings and a mantelshelf, having stained or painted these beforehand. Remember to add a ceiling coving and to make it the same as that on the walls. When everything is dry and secure, carefully glue your completed fireplace into position on the wall.

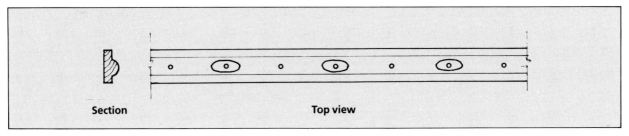

Section   **Top view**

FIG 9.4 *Embossed pattern section*

FIG 9.5 *Small fireplace*

PLAIN FIREPLACES

Although the fireplaces shown above are what we think of as Georgian, in smaller houses or in servants' quarters the fireplaces would have been made of brick, or plainly plastered with little attempt at ornamentation.

Brick fireplaces can be achieved in a number of ways – a simple method which requires some sawing is to use a piece of soft wood – whitewood or balsa – and to mark a brick or stone effect as shown in Fig 9.6. The lines should then be sawn to ⅛″ depth and the individual bricks should be cut with a lino or Stanley knife or Exacto tool. *See* Chapters 4 and 16 for alternative methods of colouring bricks and mortar.

An alternative method is to cover the wood with Tetrion to about ⅛″ thick and allow it to thicken but not set before marking out the bricks or stones with a knitting needle or similar tool. Make sure you do not go down to the wood. When dry, this can then be painted as described above.

A simple plaster finish also uses Tetrion, applied to ¹⁄₁₆″ or ⅛″ thick and smoothed over the wood. If you intend to add a mantelshelf, do this before the Tetrion sets – spread wood glue on the shelf and push it into place.

If you prefer to use polystyrene foam for your fireplace, this has the advantage of being easy to cut and mark out – it is also inexpensive, as it is used for packing everything from televisions and fridges to cutlery. Manufacturers will often supply off-cuts at a reasonable price, and you do not need to use Tetrion to simulate brick or stone – simply apply one or two coats of emulsion paint before painting in the required effect.

To etch foam, use a soldering iron with a very small bit – do not allow it to get too hot, and switch it off every three or four minutes, otherwise it will melt the foam. Use a metal ruler as a guide

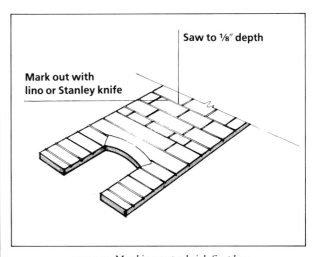

Saw to ⅛″ depth

Mark out with lino or Stanley knife

FIG 9.6 *Marking out a brick fireplace*

and gently slide the iron over biro lines previously drawn – the shapes will have to be carefully made freehand.

KITCHEN RANGE

The photographs of the interior of the country house show a kitchen range with stove, warming cupboards and warming shelves – this would originally have run on coal or wood, but might have been converted at a later date to be gas-powered, though this would not have changed the external appearance.

Fig 9.7 illustrates the general arrangement – the surround can be made from either plywood or foam sheet and finished in brick, stone or plain plaster as described above. The advantage of using wood is that the doors can be more easily hinged in place to perhaps display pies, bread, cakes or the family roast. Thin tin or aluminium sheet should be used for the metal parts.

Cut the surround from approximately 1″ thick wood or polystyrene to the exact height of the room and to the dimensions given in Fig 9.7. Glue this to a piece of strong cardboard or 1mm thick plywood or similar, as shown in Fig 9.8, and when dry, finish as described above (the area containing the shelves can be painted a plain colour if preferred). With the back facing glued in place, assemble the various shelves and bottom cross member from 1″ × ⅛″ stripwood – *see* Fig 9.9 – and glue them into position.

Next cut three pieces of tin, aluminium or litho plate as illustrated in Fig 9.10, cutting out the

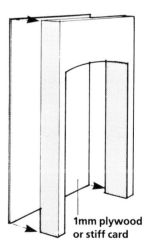

FIG 9.8 *Gluing surround to backing*

1mm plywood or stiff card

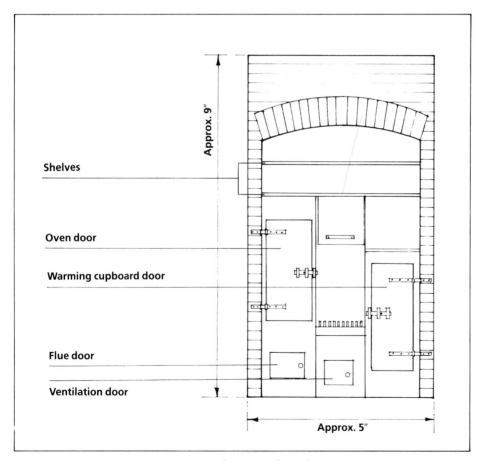

Shelves

Oven door

Warming cupboard door

Flue door

Ventilation door

Approx. 9″

Approx. 5″

FIG 9.7 *Kitchen range (front view)*

FIG 9.9 *Fitting shelves and cross members*

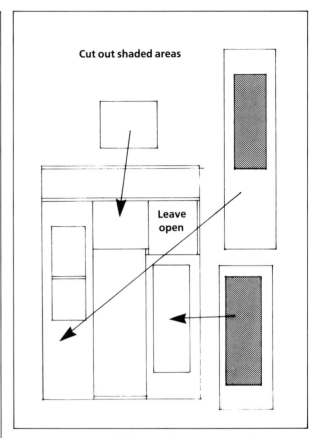

FIG 9.10 *Cutting and positioning metal*

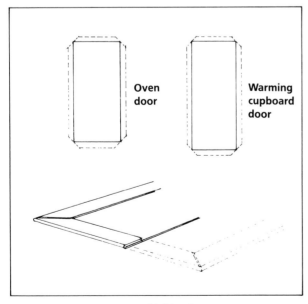

FIG 9.11 *Making doors*

centres as shown using a lino or Stanley knife – the best way to do this is to lay a piece of softwood (balsa is ideal) on the metal and cut along it. The blade can make a clean-edged cut, and there is likely to be little distortion of the metal. Refer to Fig 9.7 for where to glue the metal – the panels should completely cover the wood strips – use impact adhesive or instant glue for this.

Now make the doors for the oven and warming cupboard, as shown in Fig 9.11. These should again be made from the metal plate and should be cut ⅛″ oversize before being bent flat on the inside to provide extra strength. The corners can be cut to make a neat fold. Refer to Fig 9.12 for how to make hinges – these can be cut from the same metal sheet. When you have cut them to the shape shown, bend the hinges around a panel pin and press them into

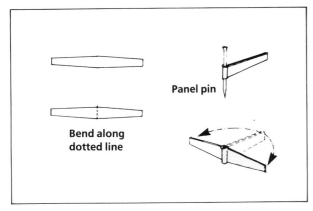

FIG 9.12 *Hinges and bolts*

FIG 9.13 *Saddles*

shape with pliers. The hinges can then be glued into place on the doors, using instant glue sparingly.

The doors will now need bolts and saddles – Fig 9.12 also shows the basic shape needed to make the bolts. Fold the metal and glue it, trimming the end

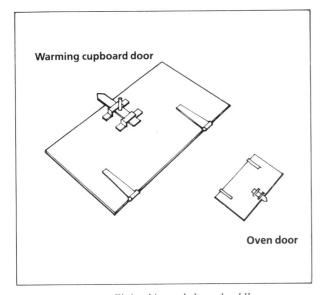

FIG 9.14 *Fitting hinges, bolts and saddles on doors*

FIG 9.15 *Kitchen range in the country house*

to produce the shape shown in Fig 9.14. When this is done, turn your attention to the saddles illustrated in Fig 9.13 – each door will need three saddles, which are bent to the shape shown. Glue one saddle to the edge of each door – *see* Fig 9.14 – and insert the pointed end of the sliding bolt. Once satisfactorily in position, the other door saddle may then be glued in place, taking care to allow the bolt to move. (The illustration shows the different positioning for the oven and cupboard doors).

Cut the heads off four panel pins and bend them carefully to the angle shown in Fig 9.16. With the doors held in place on the surround, mark out

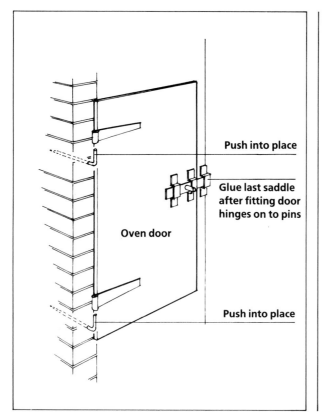

FIG 9.16 *Fitting the doors*

Push into place

Glue last saddle after fitting door hinges on to pins

Oven door

Push into place

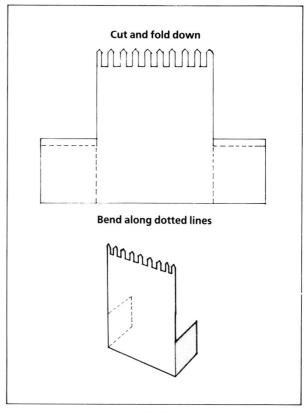

FIG 9.18 *Making a grate*

Cut and fold down

Bend along dotted lines

FIG 9.17 *Metal hood*

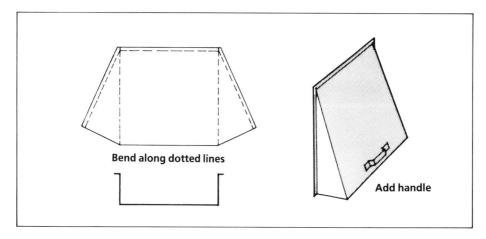

Bend along dotted lines

Add handle

FIG 9.19 *Wooden platform for coal or logs*

where to push the pins in to hold the hinges before pushing them into place. Very carefully drop the hinges on to the pins, and then glue the remaining saddle to the surround, again allowing the bolt to slide freely.

With the doors now in place, cut and bend the metal hood to the shape shown in Fig 9.17 and glue it into position above the empty space (*see* Fig 9.7). A small handle can also be cut from the metal strip and glued to the hood.

Make up the grate as illustrated in Fig 9.18, cutting the top and bending the bottom and sides to the dotted lines and gluing the sides to the front. A small piece of wood can now be cut to size and placed to bridge the side pieces – this will be a platform for coal or log effects (Fig 9.19). Make sure that the grate assembly can move easily in and out of its space. An authentic touch is to cut out and glue on false fuel ventilation doors, complete with small glued-on handles.

When everything has been glued and hung in position, all the metal parts should be painted sparingly with black eggshell paint.

FIRE BASKETS

No fireplace is ever really complete without a glowing log or coal fire – the following is a simple way to add charm to your model house.

Having measured the available space in your fireplace, first cut a piece of $\frac{1}{8}''$ plywood to a rectangle (Fig 9.20). Now cut $\frac{3}{16}''$ strips from litho plate, tin, aluminium or even straightened-out drinks cans, to overlap the plywood as shown in Fig 9.21. Cut the ends of the metal to points and fasten all the joints with instant glue – when dry, bend the legs to the shape shown in Fig 9.22 and glue them to the base of the fire basket and allow them to dry.

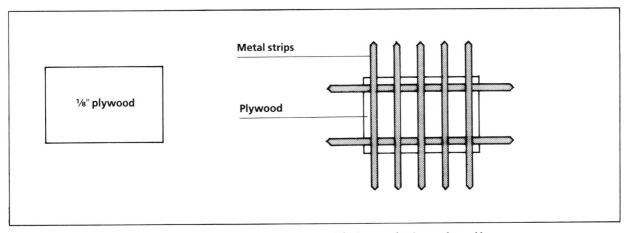

FIG 9.20 *Plywood base*　　　　FIG 9.21 *Placing metal strips on plywood base*

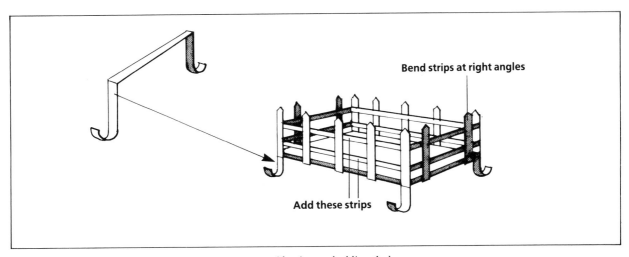

FIG 9.22 *Shaping and adding the legs*

Turn the basket over and stand it on its legs, adjusting them until the assembly is square on the ground. Bend the overlapping strips at right angles to the base and add strips around them – the result should be as illustrated in Fig 9.22.

FIG 9.23 *Grate in position in small fireplace*

COAL AND LOG FIRES

You will need fibreglass resin and fine metal mesh, both available from car accessory shops, to make up the coal or log effect. First cut a block of balsa wood higher than the basket surround and carve it into a rough dome shape – *see* Fig 9.24 – and mould

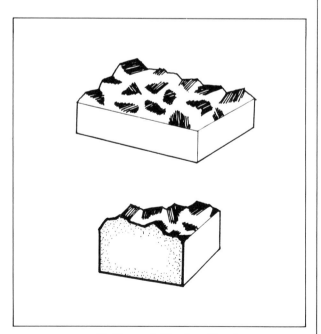

FIG 9.24 *Making coal effect from fibreglass resin and mesh*

the metal mesh around this carved block. Trim off the bottom of the mesh to the balsa and lift it off. It should now fit neatly in the fire basket – trim or adjust it to fit – and once this has been achieved, lift it out and cut a small hole in the back, large enough to allow a bulb and holder to pass through into the centre. (The middle upright at the back of the basket will have to be removed for this operation.)

Break a nugget of coal into very small pieces or use small privet branches as logs, and keep them to one side. Put the mesh back in the basket, mix up a small amount of fibreglass resin and brush or pour some over the mesh, taking care to cover it. While the resin is liquid and tacky, arrange the coal and logs on and around the exposed mesh and then pour on more resin until it is well covered – any resin that falls on to the base does not need to be removed, while any on the metal basket strips can be easily removed with acetate or nail varnish remover before it has set. Finish by painting the metalwork and underside of the base matt black.

Refer to Chapter 11 for wiring and lighting – wire up a socket and screw in a small l.e.s. bulb, and push the assembly through the hole in the back of the basket and the mesh. Some miniature manufacturers produce flickering fire effects which range from a simple unit – such as in Christmas tree sets – to more elaborate kits with between two and five bulbs and a separate flicker unit. These latter will require you to have a hollow chimney breast to accommodate the flasher unit – see the list of suppliers and stockists at the back of the book for all these effects.

Especially for fires, it is better to slightly under-power the bulbs you use – they will last much longer (maybe even indefinitely) and will save having to put wear and tear on the fire basket and carefully made mesh. Be sure also to check every joint and solder at every stage of construction, even when fitting the bulbs, as this will reduce frustration and allow you to enjoy your modelling even more.

CHAPTER TEN

STAIRCASES

$\mathscr{B}$UILDING A STAIRCASE can seem a daunting task to the novice modeller, and they are sometimes left out or built badly, thus spoiling the interior of a house. But if you want to build a house that is a model and not a toy, the staircase must be incorporated and modelled convincingly. Though staircases can be a major project in themselves, this chapter will show how they can be made with a minimum of hair-tugging.

The staircases in the country house are all made by the methods in this chapter, and we believe they are highly effective and true to the period. Some of the staircases in the other models are made from kits available from the stockists listed at the back of the book.

If highly decorative turned rails are required, this is not really possible without the aid of a miniature lathe and, of course, the skill and experience to use it. Some readers may wish to acquire this skill, but it would need a book of its own to instruct properly – such books are available, and one is on the list provided by the publisher of this book.

There is, however, an alternative available for the Georgian period, staircases produced either ready-made or in kit form – they are not cheap but they are very good interpretations, and they certainly save time. As previously mentioned, the Georgian house modeller has a lot going for him or her due to the large range of ready-made items available, but having to design or invent from scratch is extremely satisfying and more of a challenge.

SIMPLE STAIRCASES

A simple staircase can be made from triangular section wood, easily obtainable from DIY shops and shown in Fig 10.2 – the section comes in most sizes up to 1½", but for this staircase it should be somewhere between ¾" and 1" if it is to keep to scale, and the steps should be 2"–3" wide.

FIG 10.1 *Staircase with turned newel post and rails*

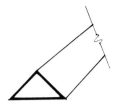

FIG 10.2 *Triangular section timber*

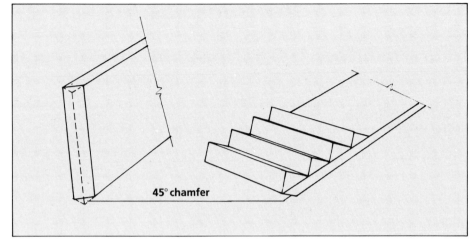

45° chamfer

FIG 10.3 *Steps glued to plywood chamfered to 45°*

The base on which the steps are mounted should be ⅛″ plywood, chamfered to 45°, as shown in Fig 10.3. Cut it to the same width as the steps, and it is better too long than too short as it can be trimmed back after the steps are glued in place.

It is essential that the staircase is constructed at 45°, as shallower or deeper angles would make the steps slope. The size of the steps will be governed by the room size – if the room is 7½″ high, 10 steps of ¾″ are required, and if the room is 8¼″ high, 11 steps of ¾″ are needed. The length of your staircase will of course be the same as the height.

When you have glued the steps to the base and all is dry, cut two triangular pieces from ¼″ plywood and glue them to the underside of the plywood base as in Fig 10.4. The final positioning of a completed staircase should be very simple, as most staircases are built against an interior wall.

It is a good idea to decide before construction whether you wish the staircase to have a handrail with open rails, as shown in Figs 10.14 and 10.15, or

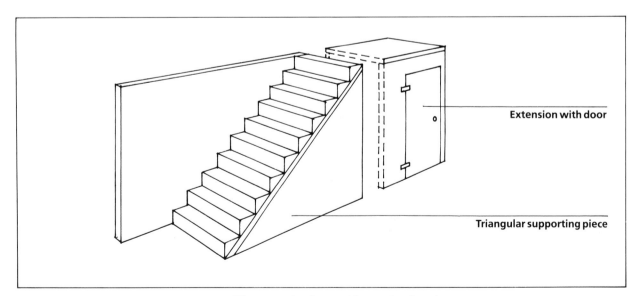

Extension with door

Triangular supporting piece

FIG 10.4 *The mounted staircase with extension for a door*

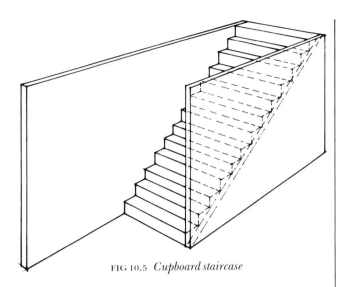

FIG 10.5 *Cupboard staircase*

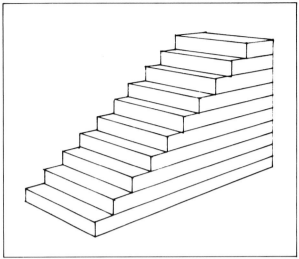

FIG 10.7 *Progressively smaller pieces of wood*

to be a cupboard staircase (Fig 10.5) – this extends to the ceiling from the first step and often incorporates a cupboard or understair door. Another option with a satisfying neatness is shown in Fig 10.4, where the plywood half wall is extended back to make room for the door.

To complete the staircase you can either paper, panel or even paint the wall.

One easy way to construct a staircase is shown in Fig 10.7, and this involves laying progressively smaller lengths of wood on top of each other and gluing them together. Use soft or hardwood for the steps, which should be cut to 2″–3″ wide and between ¾″ and 1″ deep. If you use ¾″ wood, then each piece should be ¾″ shorter than the one beneath it. Though easy, this is a heavy and rather

expensive way to construct a staircase, and has the added disadvantage that the grain of the wood will be edge on to the observer, and a thin veneer will be needed to face each riser.

Yet another method is to use identical pieces of wood – about twice the depth of the measurement required for the step or even deeper – and to nail and glue them into position as shown in Fig 10.8. One great advantage of this method is that you can change the direction of the staircase through 90° – *see* Fig 10.9 – particularly useful for difficult room sizes or for effect in a large house.

FIG 10.6 *Open and cupboard staircases*

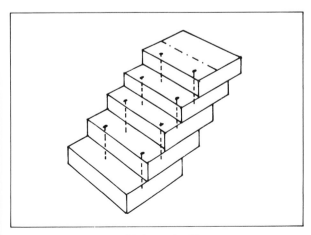

FIG 10.8 *Gluing and nailing steps*

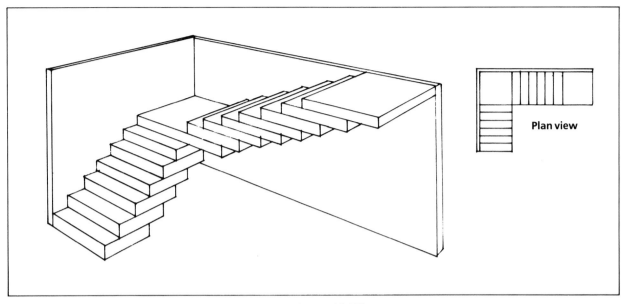

Plan view

FIG 10.9 *Staircase with 90° turn*

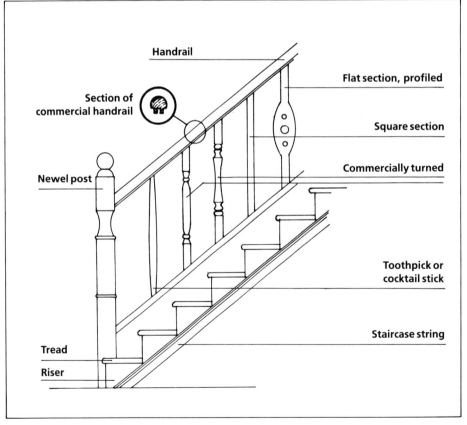

Handrail

Section of
commercial handrail

Flat section, profiled

Square section

Commercially turned

Newel post

Toothpick or
cocktail stick

Staircase string

Tread

Riser

Glue toothpick
through bead and
into stripwood,
and trim off top

Corners can
be rounded

FIG 10.10 *The parts of a staircase*

FIG 10.11 *Making a newel post*

STAIR RAILS

Stair rails add style to staircases, and a number of designs are shown below. Fig 10.10 shows the various parts of a staircase – handrails can be made from mouldings, and we recommend half round dowelling for this. Specialist miniaturist suppliers will stock more elaborate mouldings – see the list at the back of the book.

An authentic newel post can be made from a square section of stripwood and a wooden bead glued to the top with a toothpick, as shown in Fig 10.11. This can also be carved as illustrated in Figs 10.10 and 10.21.

Tread lip or nosing can be added – cut a piece of $\frac{1}{16}''$ beech or similar to about $\frac{3}{32}''$ deeper than the step, and round off the front edge. Fig 10.13 shows how to do this. Then drill holes about $\frac{1}{4}''$ from the front edge to accept the baluster rails.

For the delicate look appropriate to the Georgian and Regency periods, the rails themselves can be made from wooden cocktail sticks or toothpicks, while for a rougher cottage style, plain $\frac{1}{4}''$ square wood is effective. Both styles of rail are shown in Figs 10.14 and 10.15.

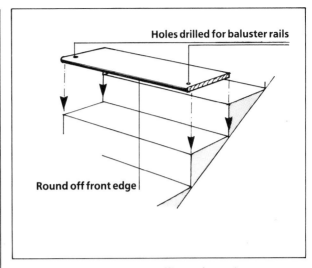

FIG 10.13 *Position of lip tread or nosing*

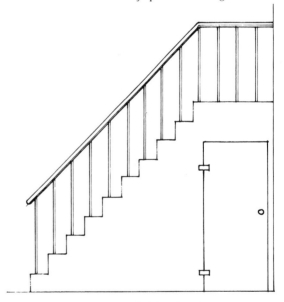

FIG 10.14 *Toothpick-style rails*

FIG 10.12 *Making a staircase*

You will need accuracy and a lot of patience to fit the cocktail sticks or toothpicks, as the holes in the stairs must be made by holding a drill absolutely vertical. This is best done by using a miniature drill stand. The handrail must also be drilled at an angle, as can be seen in Figs 10.14 and 10.15, so you will need a steady hand.

Assuming, however, that you have drilled each stair accurately, and that all the uprights stand

59

FIG 10.15 *Square section rails*

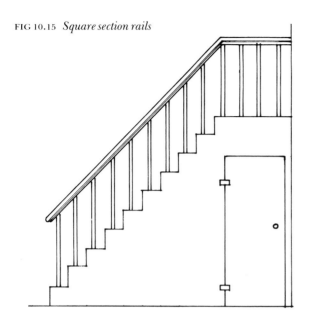

absolutely straight in line when in place, it is possible to avoid having to drill the handrail – although this also is a painstaking method and not much simpler than drilling. Having removed any sharp edges from the uprights and ensuring that they are all exactly the same height, glue the handrail into place using a fast-drying glue such as Superglue.

Square section wood is easy to use (even if the end result is quite crude), as the rails can be glued throughout – the larger area makes it possible for the glue to get a better purchase and make a good bond.

Cut all the rails to the same height and ensure that the cut ends are completely flat – cut the top end diagonally at 45° as shown in Fig 10.16, so that the rails join the steps and handrail accurately. Glue each rail into position on the stairs, making quite sure that it is vertical from all angles, and when dry glue the handrail into place as before.

Square section rails can be made more elegant and attractive by being carved – *see* Fig 10.16. Simply take off a thin sliver from each edge to within ¼″ of the top and bottom of the rail, then notch the wood all round to a depth of no more than 1/16″ on ¼″ square section and 1/32″ on 1/8″ square section wood.

An authentic-looking rail can be made from a small block (1½″ × ½″) of hardwood, though any wood will do, using a fretsaw or by hand carving. Mark the wood as shown in Fig 10.18, and drill through with a large bit for the centre hole and a smaller bit for the others. Hold the block in a vice and cut out and carve the wood as illustrated, remembering to angle the top as shown in Fig 10.16 – this is best done before starting to carve. When the shape has been cut, saw it into 1/8″ strips – 10–11 identical rails can be cut from a 1½″ block – *see* Fig 10.19. Glue the completed rails on to each step,

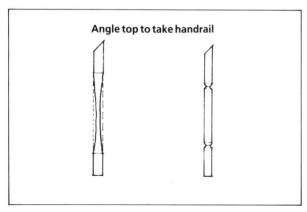

Angle top to take handrail

FIG 10.16 *Carved rails*

FIG 10.17 *Plain and carved rails*

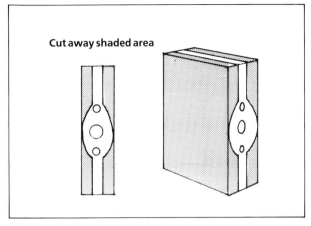

FIG 10.18 *Marked block for decorative rails*

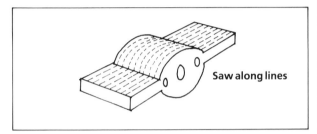

FIG 10.19 *Ready for sawing*

FIG 10.20 *Decorative rails in place*

check that they are all straight and true, and then glue on the handrail, with the result as shown in Fig 10.20.

Towards the end of the 18th century staircases of beautiful design and craftsmanship became common in the houses of the well-to-do. Mouldings, staircase strip and strings, treads, risers, nosings, newel posts and all the various components can either be bought in kit form or ready-made from the specialists listed in the back, enabling you to produce exactly the kind of staircase you want for your model.

FIG 10.21 *A decorative staircase*

CHAPTER ELEVEN

WIRING
AND LIGHTING

*I*LLUMINATION IN GEORGIAN HOUSES differed little from that of previous eras – oil-powered lamps and candles were all that were available until gas and (later) electricity came on the scene, so the following paragraphs are confined to the early forms of lighting. Obviously if a period house of up to the Regency time is to be furnished and lit authentically, gas or electricity would be totally inappropriate – but if the model you build is meant to represent a period house lived in at the present time, then modern-day fittings can be utilised.

All the lighting shown in this chapter can be made quite easily by the methods described. It is highly effective, as the photographs of the country house show, and can be used in any of the plans in this book.

If, however, ready-made light fittings are preferred, an impressive range of electrical fittings is available – addresses of suppliers and stockists are given in the back of the book. The one possible disadvantage is that they may be quite expensive.

BASIC LIGHTING

An inexpensive way of lighting is to use old Christmas tree lighting sets, making sure that they employ the screw-in bulbs and not the push-fit type – my daughter and I use these lights as they have an old-fashioned look to them. Specialist shops sell the candle type of bulb, but again these are expensive and the round bulbs are cheaper (*see* Fig 11.1). To re-use Christmas tree lights, remove the shade and push the socket out, then unsolder the joint with a soldering iron – put the hot iron to the soldered joint and pull the wire free.

Any colour on the old bulbs can be removed by dipping the bulb in nail varnish remover or paint thinner. Make a note of the size of the bulb set if you intend to re-use the bulbs – they are usually 20- or 40-light sets, and the voltage required will be different. 20 lights run on 12.5 volts and 40 lights

FIG 11.1 *A dramatic use of lighting*

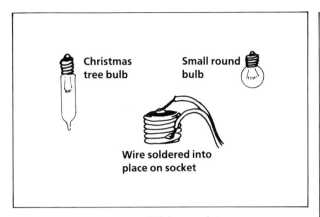

FIG 11.2 *Wiring a socket*

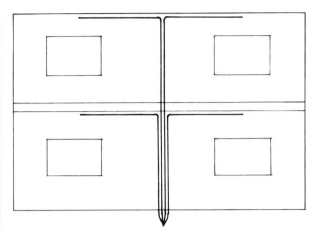

FIG 11.3 *Wiring plan for four bulbs*

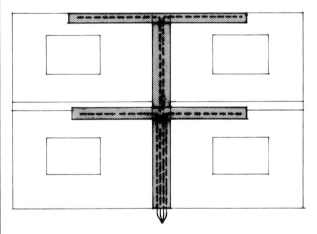

FIG 11.4 *Concealing wires on a plywood house*

run on 7.5 volts – pages 68 and 69 give details of transformers.

Fig 11.2 shows how to wire up a socket. You will need fine two-core wiring, available from model and miniaturist shops or perhaps from a local electrical supplier. Simply solder one wire to the small dimple at the top of the socket and the other to the side casing.

When fitting the wiring to the house, leave at least 12″ of cable from each socket at the back of the house – this will have to be joined together when you have finished putting the lighting in place (*see* pages 64 and 65).

In a house with foam walls, cut a groove in the wall to take the cable and then plaster over the cable. If the house is made from plywood, then the wires will have to be permanently taped into place with masking tape, which can then be plastered over or covered with textured paint – Fig 11.3 shows how the wiring for four bulbs runs down the back of the house, while Fig 11.4 illustrates how to conceal the wires on a plywood house.

When all the lights are in place, join the cable ends as shown in Fig 11.5, either by soldering them together or using a connector – if you use the latter method, attach two further cables to one side of the connector and solder the other end to the jack plug. This method is suitable for a simple house requiring only four to six lights – houses of six or seven rooms will need a large number of lights for the hallways and extra lighting in each room, and, though it is possible to connect eight bulbs in this way, joining the cable becomes progressively more complicated as more lights are added.

METHODS OF WIRING

We recommend lighting in parallel, as this method means that if one bulb should fail, no other bulbs will go out and it is easy to replace. With the other method, wiring in series, should one bulb fail all the others will go out, and it is a time-consuming and temper-trying business to trace the faulty bulb.

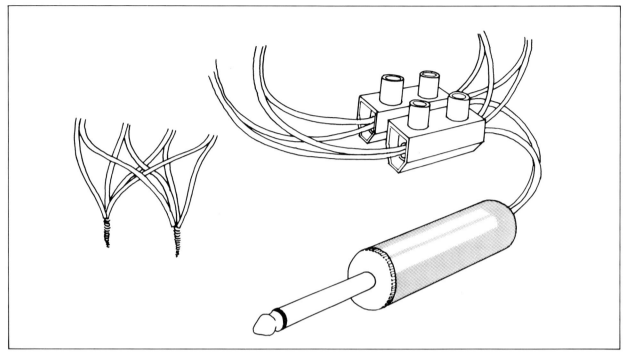

FIG 11.5 *Joining cables*

FIG 11.6 *Plain kitchen lighting*

Both kinds are shown in Fig 11.7, as is the third method, a combination of lighting in parallel and in series – refer back to Fig 11.2 for how to wire the sockets.

After soldering the wire to the holder, make sure that a suitable length of wire is left over for attaching to the ring main – a simplified system of that used in full-sized house lighting.

For the main cable, you should use 2-amp 2-core wire – avoid using ultra-fine wire as this is difficult to use – and 2-core fine lighting wire for attaching

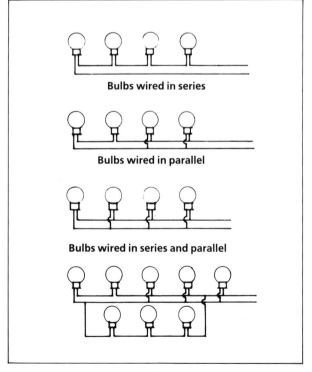

Bulbs wired in series

Bulbs wired in parallel

Bulbs wired in series and parallel

FIG 11.7 *Wiring bulbs*

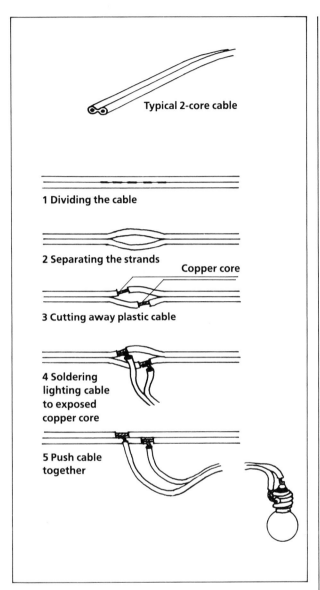

Typical 2-core cable

1 Dividing the cable

2 Separating the strands

Copper core

3 Cutting away plastic cable

4 Soldering lighting cable to exposed copper core

5 Push cable together

FIG 11.8 *Attaching lighting wires*

other and the two strands can be pushed together without insulation.

Connect the cable to a jack plug, which will then connect to a socket from the chosen transformer (*see* page 68) – this method means that as many lights as necessary can be tapped in, providing the number is compatible with the amperage of the transformer. Fig 11.9 illustrates this. It is also possible to connect the cable to a toggle switch, the kind used on reading lamps, before leading it to the transformer.

For foam walls, you will need to cut grooves in the tops of the back walls to hold the cable and then hold the cable in position with masking tape before plastering and painting or covering with wallpaper – *see* Fig 11.10. In a house made from plywood, you will need hollowed-out ceiling coving

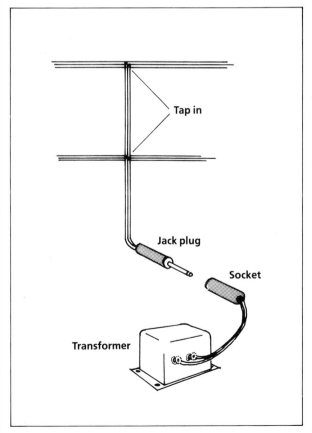

Tap in

Jack plug

Socket

Transformer

FIG 11.9 *Connecting to a transformer*

the sockets at the main tap-in points. Fig 11.8 shows the procedure for attaching the wires – carefully split the two wires of the main cable at each tap-in point (every 1″ or 1½″) with a razorblade or lino knife, and separate the two strands. Cut away the plastic sheathing, taking care not to cut through the copper core, and solder a strand of the fine wire to each exposed copper core. If the joins are placed as shown, they will not be touching each

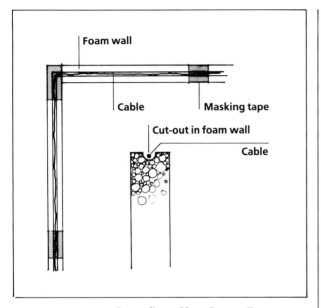

FIG 11.10 *Concealing cable on foam walls*

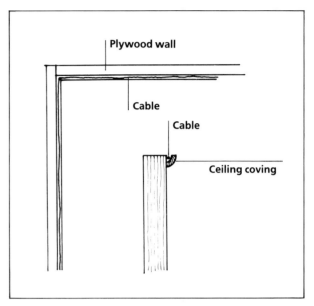

FIG 11.12 *Concealing cable on plywood walls*

to hide the cable – this coving can be obtained from DIY shops, and the method is shown in Fig 11.12.

You should now give some thought to the kind of shade you wish to use. The shades from an old Christmas tree set may be suitable – one type of these is shown in Fig 11.13 – they are usually coloured and translucent, and look good if sprayed bronze. Alternatively, many different light fittings and shades of all styles are available from suppliers. However, we believe that the greatest satisfaction can be gained from making your own shades and fittings from cheap, commonly available materials,

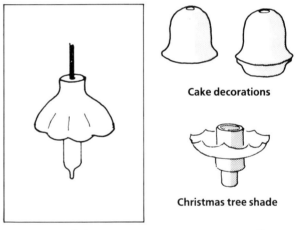

FIG 11.13 *Christmas tree shade and bulb*

FIG 11.14 *Easily made shades*

as shown in Fig 11.14 – and apart from Christmas tree lights, there are also cake decorations and 'wedding bells'.

It is possible to buy wall-mounted light switches and sockets, but these can look out of scale in a model house. If you wish to use these – for a table lamp, for instance – you will need to hide them behind pieces of furniture or at the side of a chimney breast nearest the back of the house.

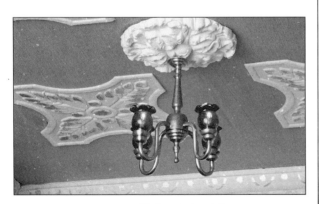

FIG 11.11 *Elaborate chandelier*

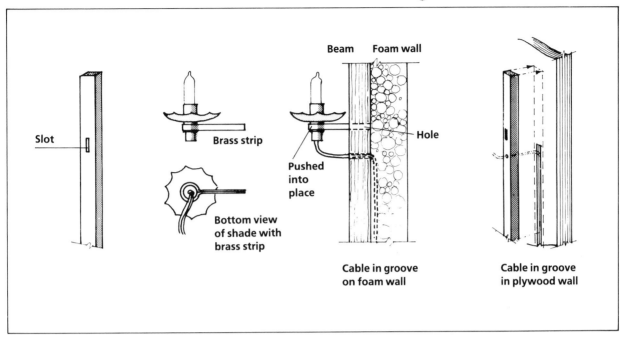

FIG 11.15 *Fitting wall lights*

CEILING LIGHTS

The cable running along the ceiling is often difficult to conceal, particularly when a plywood ceiling is being used. The grain does not always run in the same direction on plywood, which is multi-layered, and this means that an attempt to groove the ceiling could end disastrously with your cutting right through the plywood and having to start that ceiling/floor again from the beginning.

A safe and simple method is to secure the cable in position with masking tape and then paint the ceiling with two coats of textured emulsion paint, *avoiding the masking tape*. Apply a further coat, to both ceiling and masking tape this time, and this should hide the cable. Covering the ceiling with Anaglypta embossed paper will also cover the tape, but you must either cut the paper or make a hole for the cable very accurately. The alternative is to plaster the ceiling, but this can be messy.

You can either buy or make ceiling roses – if you decide on the latter course, a good way is to use buttons upside down and plastered to the ceiling, afterwards drilling a hole to house the wiring. The possibilities are endless, and your imagination will lead you to find alternatives.

WALL LIGHTS

For plywood walls, the same method can be used as for a ceiling – covering the cable with masking tape and then using textured paint. Make sure that the wall surface is smooth before adding any wallpaper. For foam walls, the easiest method is to attach the fitting to a thin beam, which is then let into a groove in the wall. Refer to Fig 11.15, which shows how to wrap ¼″ brass strip round the light socket and push it into the slot in the beam, fixing it with glue. The wire goes through a hole drilled beneath the slot and is laid along the groove running down the beam, which is then glued in place.

TRANSFORMERS

Transformers vary in price depending on the output of the unit. For a unit running four to six bulbs a minimum output of 500 milliamps will be needed and if the bulbs used are 12 volt then a 12-volt transformer will be required. If more bulbs are wanted, then a transformer with a minimum of 1 amp output will be required, and we have successfully run 17 bulbs with such a transformer. If the bulbs you are using are 6 or 7.5 volts, then a transformer rated at 6 volts should be used.

It is very difficult to obtain a 1 amp transformer exept by mail order or from a miniaturist shop (*see* page 160). Smaller powered transformers can usually be purchased from hi-fi shops and they are all of the three-pin plug-in variety.

A similar type of transformer is also available from the same outlets and this has a variable voltage switch giving a choice of, say, 2–12 volts, but the milliamp output is usually quite small and is therefore only suitable for a maximum of four bulbs.

All the above information relates to bulbs wired in parallel, but if you decide to wire in series then a smaller transformer will suffice. Any number of bulbs can be used in this way on transformers that give an output of only 60 milliamps.

Below are details of various transformers and their uses.

For 12-volt bulbs and a 12-volt transformer

No. of bulbs	How wired	Minimum transformer output in milliamps
1	Alone	60
3	Parallel	180
Any number	Series	60
1 plus any number	Parallel Series	120
3 plus 4	Parallel Series	240
10	Parallel	600

Assuming that most model builders will opt for the parallel method of wiring, a practical guide to choice of transformer would be as follows: for 6 or 7.5 volt bulbs, use a 6-volt transformer; for 12 or

FIG 11.16 *Wall sconces*

12.5 volt bulbs, use a 12-volt transformer. A transformer with an output of 500 milliamps would light between 1 and 6 bulbs; a 1 amp transformer would power up to 16 bulbs; a 1.5 amp transformer would be suitable for very large houses with perhaps up to 24 bulbs. It is better to underpower the transformer so that it will last longer and this is usually done by using fewer bulbs, i.e. 6×60 milliamps = 360 milliamps, but use a 500 milliamp transformer.

Model house lighting should never be wired to the mains. The use of a transformer is essential.

The methods I describe here are relatively simple and inexpensive. The reader will no doubt have noticed that keeping costs down is easy with a bit of improvisation, as do-it-yourself methods are quite substantially cheaper than using ready-made fittings or wiring kits. To give the reader a choice, however, details of one of the most popular wiring kits are given below.

The most popular kits are the 'copper tape' ones which are nearly always rated at 12 volts. The kit comprises a number of yards of copper foil tape which comes in various widths but usually $^3/_{16}''$. It also includes a few reusable plugs, a test bulb and brass connector nails.

The copper tape has a self-adhesive backing and can be stuck to any clean surface. The maximum amperage is five amps. Once you have decided where the lights are going to be placed the positions should be marked on the walls or ceilings in pencil and the copper tape should then be pressed into

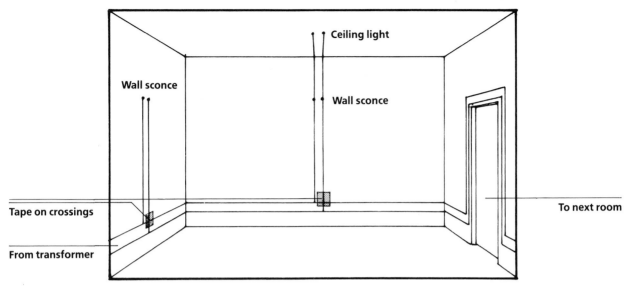

FIG 11.17 *Copper tape in position*

place. Two lines of tape are required and these should be about ⅛″ apart, as shown in Fig 11.17.

Care should be taken when fixing the tape as the most common cause of short circuits is the two tapes touching. Another common cause is a bad connection or break in the tape.

If for any reason the tapes have to cross each other, say for a wall sconce, then a small piece of clear (or insulating) tape should be used to stop a short circuit. For joins, the tape must be pierced with a sharp tool or a brass nail through both strips. The circuits should be tested one by one before the room is decorated to ensure that enough power is available. Wires from the lamps must be securely attached to the tape, and this is done by twisting or soldering the wires to brass nails which are then hammered directly into the copper tape. The plugs provided with the kit may be used for wall or ceiling lights as follows: strip off ½″ of insulation from the lamp wires and pass through the top and bottom centre holes of the plug. From the base, push one wire through each of the two outer holes until ¼″ of bare wire protrudes, then bend them over and secure them. Place the plug over the copper tape

so that one wire touches each tape and trim any slack wire. Insert a brass nail into each of the small holes and push the nail home: this will secure the plug to the tape. Any loose wire around the nail should be cut off. Gently pull out slack wires and snap the top shut.

BULBS

My daughter and I feel that reliability in light fittings is an absolute must, and we have little confidence in bulbs that cannot be changed. Some commercially-produced fittings have such bulbs, necessitating the removal and replacement of the entire fitting – not only difficult, but expensive.

The type of bulb usually found in this kind of fitting is called a 'grain of wheat', a very thin bulb, illustrated in Fig 11.18. The better commercially manufactured fittings incorporate removable bulbs, which are long-lasting and reliable. There are two different types: the first has two prongs at the end of the bulb which slot into two holes provided in the bulb holder; the second type is a very small screw-in bulb, which obviously just screws into the light fitting. Both types are also shown in Fig 11.18.

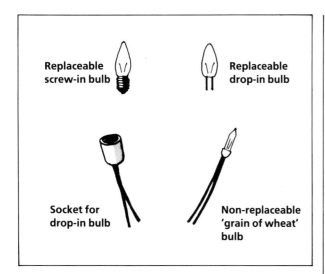

FIG 11.18 *Replaceable and non-replaceable bulbs*

Sockets and bulbs for the DIY enthusiast can be purchased from specialist shops. These bulbs can be used in the fittings we have shown in this chapter, and examples are shown in the photographs of the country house.

SHADES AND FITTINGS

If you are unable to get hold of Christmas tree light shades as described above, birthday cake candle holders painted gold or bronze make very good shades, especially for wall sconces. I also like to use home-made lanterns made from litho plate or thin aluminium, shown in Fig 11.19. The basic shape can be cut out with scissors, but the cut-outs must be carefully done with an Exacto tool or lino or Stanley knife.

Fig 11.19 illustrates the parts of the lantern – one piece of metal is folded three times as shown, to make four sides, and a square of balsa wood is cut to fit into the top of the shade. Sand the top and drill a hole for the wire in the centre before making a larger hole for the bulb holder in the bottom.

We often make a wall-mounted light by cutting a small bracket from copper or brass strip (available from model shops) – not aluminium, as this cannot be soldered – and bending it at right angles before spot-soldering it to the socket – *see* Fig 11.21. When fitting this light as described above, you can put it to any angle you wish, and if you use a Christmas tree light without a shade, this can look effective as a candle. Alternatively, you can use l.e.s. bulbs in these lights.

LANTERNS

An authentic-looking lantern is easy to make using some large cup washers, available from DIY shops in packets of ten or so. They are hollow underneath and most often come in a brass finish. Fig 11.22 illustrates the method: cut a small oblong shape of c' ar celluloid sheet and wrap it round a piece of dowelling the same diameter as the inside rim of the cup washer, including a small overlap.

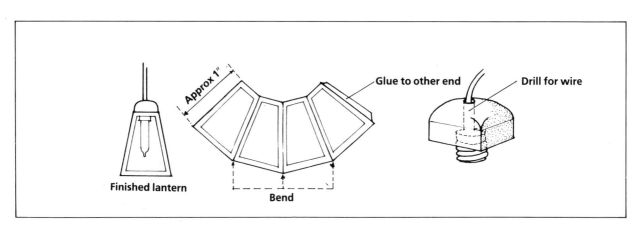

FIG 11.19 *Lantern*

FIG 11.20 *Hall light*

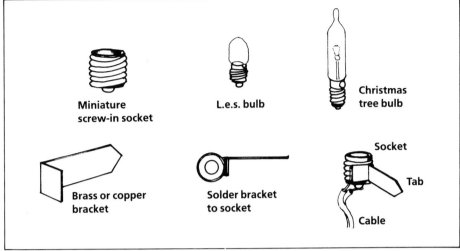

FIG 11.21 *Wall-mounted light fitting*

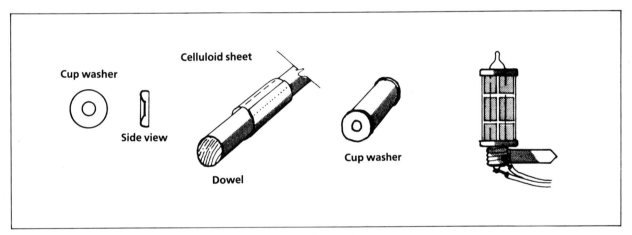

FIG 11.22 *Lantern light*

Glue the celluloid into a tube using instant glue or balsa cement before cutting the tube you have made about ⅛″ shorter than a Christmas tree bulb – the tip of the bulb should project as in the illustration. Glue the celluloid tube into the underside of each cup washer with instant glue, and when it has dried, drop the shade over the bulb. Paint on framing or use pinstripe tape.

This is just one of the ways you can use household objects to create an original and satisfying piece for your model – imagination and experiment will produce unique results.

FIG 11.23 *Outside light*

CHAPTER TWELVE

ROOFING

T HERE ARE TWO MATERIALS from which roofs can be made – plywood and thick card or cardboard. The main difference is that card or cardboard should not be used for roofs that open, but apart from this they are quite effective and much cheaper than plywood. It is imperative to support cardboard roofs at regular intervals to avoid sagging, especially after they have been decorated – look at Fig 12.2 for the positioning of foam or plywood interior walls which will support even a large roof. Remember to cut a notch in the apex of the walls to take the master beam.

Either material can be finished in a number of ways, ranging from the simple to the complicated. At the simple end, and best used on childrens' dolls' houses, *not* the models in this book, you can paint the roof panels with a coat of undercoat and then with a topcoat of slate grey before marking the roof tiles with a black felt-tip pen.

TILING

Fig 12.3 shows how to produce a simple and effective tiled roof using sheets of fine emery paper. Cut them into strips and then cut them halfway

FIG 12.1 *Tiles and dormer windows*

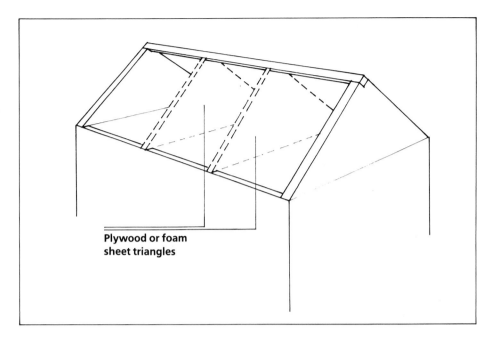

FIG 12.2 *Roof supports*

**Plywood or foam
sheet triangles**

through at tile-width intervals, which will be any-thing from ¾″ to 1″ if they are to be scaled down to size. *After* fixing on the guttering (see Chapter 13) and starting from the bottom of the roof, glue each strip on to the roof.

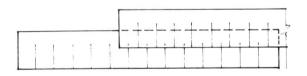

FIG 12.3 *Cutting and arranging tiling strips*

Each succeeding course should be glued on as indicated by the dotted lines in Fig 12.3, with the 'tiles' overlapping the divisions and alternating each vertical cut. The strips should be completely covered with glue to prevent the edges or corners lifting, and the highest strip should be covered by ridge tiles cut out as illustrated in Fig 12.4.

Bend along — — V V V V V — **dotted line**

FIG 12.4 *Ridge tiles cut out*

The finished emery paper roof will benefit from two or three coats of clear matt varnish to take away the abrasiveness – the varnish is long-lasting and easy to apply. If the emery paper is well covered but does not look too even, the result will look good for a very small outlay. The same technique can also be used with thick black paper, available from most art shops or office suppliers. Using matt paper and the same varnishing, a realistic finish can be obtained.

Office suppliers also stock stiff card – although more expensive, this can provide an excellent sur-face and has the advantage of being available in a series of colours, some of which – the reds and browns – can be used for stone roofs. If you decide to use this, make sure that the colour goes all the way through the card – if the centre is white, this will show up when the card is cut, and will render your work futile.

When making a stone-type roof for your model, remember that stone tiling was always smaller than slate tiling, and you will need to correspondingly make the tile cuts considerably smaller than those mentioned above.

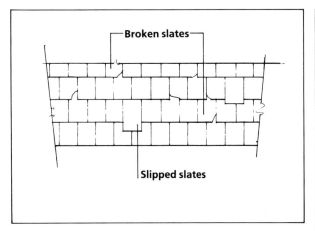

FIG 12.5 *Weathered tiles*

Authentic effects of age can be achieved on any of the above finishes by 'weathering' the slates. Fig 12.5 has examples of how cracked, slipped and broken tiles or rough edges can be used in the courses – although it will take longer, the results will show that such attention to detail is well worth persevering with.

The true perfectionist may construct the roof just like that of a full-sized house, using roof trusses and battens and attaching each tile separately.

Though satisfying, this method is extremely time-consuming and is rarely encountered outside showpiece or museum-standard houses – and though not too difficult for an experienced modeller, it can be expensive, especially if miniature scale tiles and slates are to be used.

ROOFS THAT OPEN

Plywood roofs can easily be hinged to allow them to be raised to show attic rooms or roof space. The most often used and best hinge for the purpose is piano hinge – the thinner the better – which is screwed into position on the underside of the opening roof panel as shown in Fig 12.6. If the ridge beam is reasonably thick (at least ¾″ square), there will be enough to screw into on the house side before you glue and panel-pin the rear section into place. Piano hinge is also recommended for hinging the front panels of model houses, and can be purchased from the stockists listed at the back of the book.

Of course, if you have an opening roof, you will find that emery or card ridge tiles will not suit the purpose, as the ridge tiles will need to be flexible.

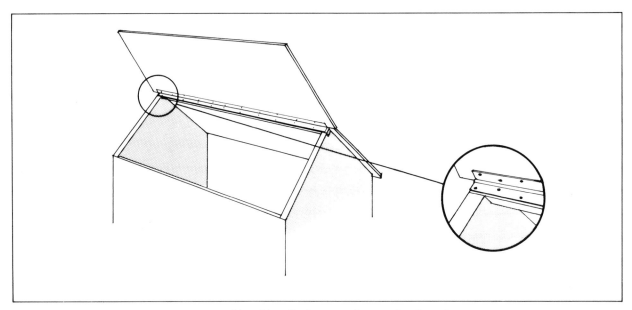

FIG 12.6 *Piano hinge fixed to master beam and roof panel*

FIG 12.7 *Roof tiles and brick side panel*

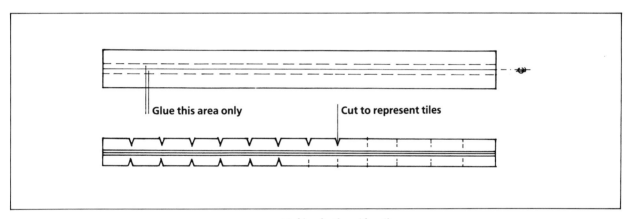

Glue this area only

Cut to represent tiles

FIG 12.8 *Making leather ridge tiles*

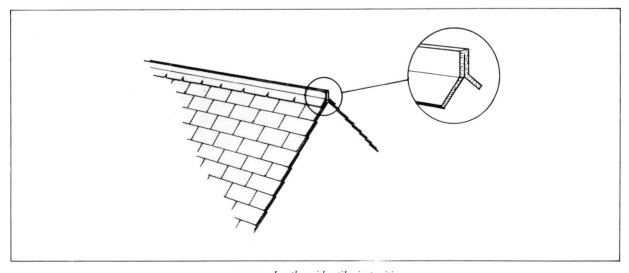

FIG 12.9 *Leather ridge tiles in position*

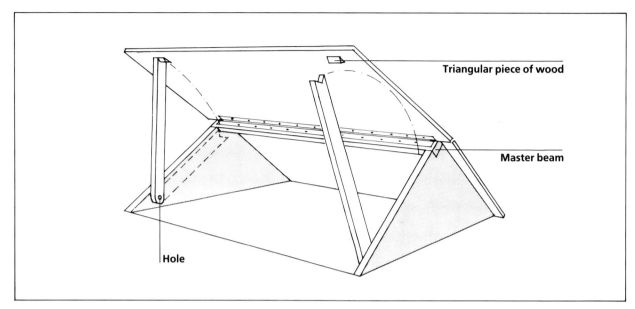

FIG 12.10 *Roof stays*

One good solution is to use a strip of fairly stiff leather as sold in habadashery shops for repairing worn jacket cuffs – this usually comes in the right width, about 1½″.

Lay the leather strip shiny side down and draw a line exactly down the centre with a biro. Apply Evostik adhesive about ⅛″ on either side of the line as shown in Fig 12.8, and double the leather strip over the line and allow it to dry. Using a pair of sharp scissors, carefully cut out notches to represent tiles down either side, and when you have completed the slating and have glued and panel-pinned the roof panels into place, glue the ridge tile into position as shown in Fig 12.9, again using Evostik or an impact glue. The leather strip will overlay the last course of tiles on both roof panels and hide the hinge, while the first glued area will stand up, giving a flexible and good-looking row of ridge slates. Most importantly, the free working of the hinge will be unaffected.

ROOF STAYS

An open roof needs roof stays. Glue two small triangular pieces of wood to the inside of the roof as shown in Fig 12.10 before cutting the two shapes shown in the illustration from a piece of ⅜″ × ¼″

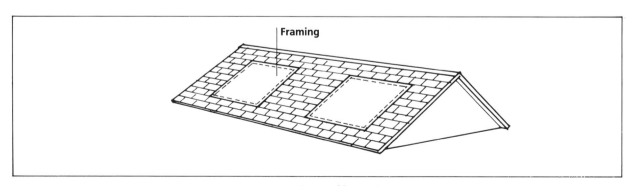

FIG 12.11 *Removable panels*

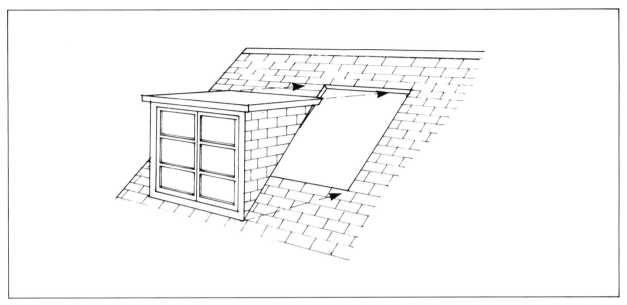

FIG 12.12 *Removable attic dormer windows*

hardwood strip. These shapes must be able to fold flat into the roof, and be no longer than indicated by the dotted line. Now carefully drill a small hole – about $^3/_{16}$″ – through the bottom of each stay and fix them with small screws to the inside of the roof. The stays will then be retained by the two triangular pieces of wood on the roof.

REMOVABLE ROOFS

An alternative to the lifting roof is to make all or part of it removable – not an ideal solution, but one with the virtue of simplicity. The three methods shown here are easy to achieve.

Fig 12.11 shows two large cut-outs which are used as simple removable panels. The dotted lines indicate basic framing to prevent the panels falling through.

If you wish to elaborate on this method, you can make attic dormer windows (see Chapter 6) to fit on to the cut-outs, as shown in Fig 12.12.

The simplest solution is to make the whole roof removable. For this to be achieved, the roof has to be built strongly – the side walls and roof panels must be thick enough and panel-pinned and glued

properly, to avoid a warped final assembly. The roof is positioned on top of the main house structure as seen in Fig 12.13.

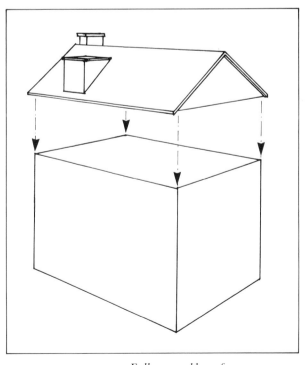

FIG 12.13 *Fully removable roof*

CHAPTER THIRTEEN

GUTTERS
AND DOWNSPOUTS

GUTTERS AND DOWNSPOUTS should be incorporated into any model house with a claim to authenticity, as by the Georgian period they were established features. They are not difficult to construct and fit.

GUTTERS

For simple but convincing guttering, cut a 2″ wide strip the length of your house from a sheet of 22 swg thin metal – this can be tin or litho plate,

FIG 13.1 *Minor pipes and main downspout*

aluminium or even a carefully straightened out beer or soft drink can. Place the strip on a smooth straight surface – a table or workbench is ideal – and extend it over the edge by about ½″.

Place a length of ⅜″ dowelling (slightly longer than the metal strip) along the edge of the table or bench as shown in Fig 13.2. Hold the dowel in place with your fingers and carefully fold the metal about halfway round it, working towards each end of the metal strip. Press firmly along the entire length of the metal with a smooth instrument such as a spoon handle to achieve an even bend – *see* Fig 13.3.

If the roof is at approximately 45°, the angle of the metal to the roof should be as shown in Fig 13.4, but if the roof angle is shallower than 45°, you will need to bend the metal to the shape shown in Fig 13.5. (This will ensure that the side of the gutter is horizontal.) After you have put the initial curve on the metal, hold the dowel in place, put the metal strip on the flat surface and press evenly along the length of the strip until the correct shape is achieved.

Now glue the gutter section to the roof with an impact adhesive such as Evostik – if the roof is made of cardboard, you will find that the gutter gives it a good deal of strengthening and reinforcement.

Form the gutter ends by gluing small sections of ⅜″ half round beading about ⅛″ thick to the ends with impact adhesive or Superglue. The final touch is to make joints from ⅛″ wide pieces of the strip metal and glue them to the underside of the gutter

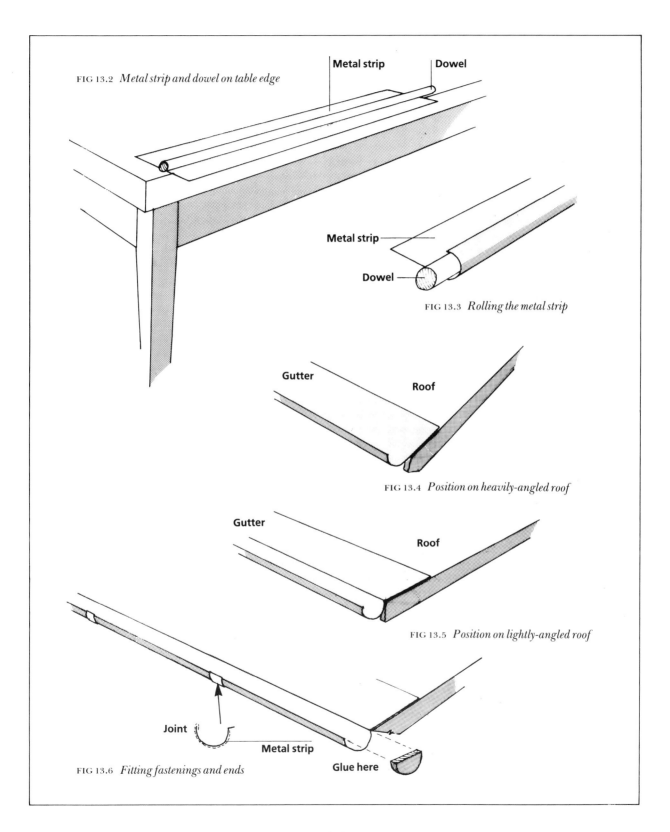

FIG 13.2 *Metal strip and dowel on table edge*

Metal strip

Dowel

Metal strip

Dowel

FIG 13.3 *Rolling the metal strip*

Gutter

Roof

FIG 13.4 *Position on heavily-angled roof*

Gutter

Roof

FIG 13.5 *Position on lightly-angled roof*

Joint

Metal strip

Glue here

FIG 13.6 *Fitting fastenings and ends*

FIG 13.7 *Downspout in place*

as shown in Fig 13.6, again using instant glue or impact adhesive. You can then begin adding the slating as described in Chapter 12.

DOWNSPOUTS

There are two types of downspout – a main downspout will run down the side of the house and can be made from ⅜″ dowel, while a minor pipe runs down the side of attic windows and should be made from ¼″ dowel.

Assuming that the main downspout is to run straight down the side of the house as in Fig 13.9, cut the dowel to a length from the gutter to about ½″ from the base of the model. Carefully cut a hollow from the top of the dowel so that it will fit the underside of the gutter and cut the bottom of the dowel at an angle to allow an outlet joint to be made. Use the cut-off piece to form the outlet and remember to glue it on facing the right way round – a further effect can be obtained by drilling out the centre of the outlet dowel.

A similar technique can be used to make angled joints if these are needed just below the gutter – *see* Fig 13.9. This needs care and accuracy, and you will have to cut new pieces of dowel to the correct angles.

To fix the downspout to the house wall, cut a 2″ length of ½″ masking or PVC tape and wrap it carefully round the dowel in the place where you want the fastening point to be – *see* Fig 13.9. (Two or three fastening points are the norm, but it will ultimately depend on your choice and size of house.) For a really authentic look, add a further band of tape, this time 2″ × ¼″, on top of the other tape along the dotted line, as again illustrated in Fig 13.9.

To fit the downspout to the house, drill a ¹⁄₁₆″ hole through the centre of the tape joint to take a panel pin (1¼″ is the usual length) and push the pin through. When you have decided how far away from the house you wish the downspout to be, cut a piece of plastic or brass tubing to that length and

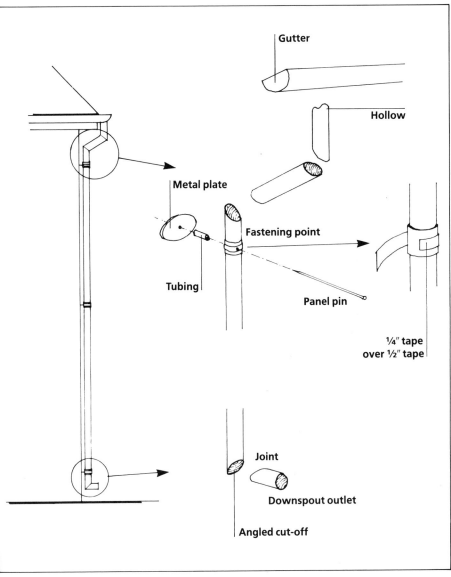

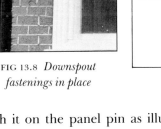

FIG 13.8 *Downspout fastenings in place*

FIG 13.9 *Downspout details*

push it on the panel pin as illustrated. For additional scale effect, cut a small plate of thin metal, again as shown in Fig 13.9, drill a small hole in the centre and push the pin through it.

Before hammering the panel pins home into the wall, drill a slightly undersized hole for the pin – this also applies to high-density foam. Make sure that the pins do not penetrate through to the inside of the walls on an all-plywood house.

It is also a good idea to paint all round the downspout and fastenings before fixing them to the house. Matt black is the best finish, but if you decide to use gloss, remember to undercoat the dowel first.

Gutterings and downspouts can, of course, be purchased ready-made, and there are alternative methods and materials of producing them – plastic tubes and empty ballpoint pen casings are among these, but the final choice is up to you, the builder.

CHAPTER FOURTEEN

RAILINGS

MANY FINE EXAMPLES of balcony railings are available ready-made from the manufacturers listed at the back of the book. However, while most of the intricate wrought iron variety are virtually impossible for the average modeller to produce, simple railings can be made using easily obtainable materials and a minimum of specialised tools.

GARDEN RAILS

The garden rails shown in the photographs of the town house are made from strip metal and wooden cocktail sticks, although plastic or bone cocktail sticks are also good for this purpose and some of the plastic ones may have a square section in the middle, adding to the decorative effect. Toothpicks are generally smaller than cocktail sticks, but should be long enough for most railings.

The strip metal can be aluminium, brass or copper and the railings shown are built on top of a brick-finished piece of wood about ¾″ thick and about four bricks high, with a half round cement finish, illustrated in Fig 14.2.

Although the strip metal can be of virtually any type, it must be no more than ³⁄₁₆″–¼″ wide and approximately ¹⁄₁₆″ thick. Experiments have proved

FIG 14.1 *Railings on walls and steps*

FIG 14.2 *Wall prepared with cement finish*

that old umbrella ribs are very good – these come already made into a U-section and have the advantage of being rigid and looking excellent when made up and painted.

The strip should be cut to the exact length of the railings required and should then be held in the correct position on the wall or yard or base with masking tape as shown in Fig 14.3. Then, using a drill bit as close to the diameter of the toothpick or cocktail stick as possible, drill through the metal strip into the wood to a depth of about ½″ – on a flat base, this will need to be no deeper than the wood itself. Drill the holes at regular intervals and then remove the masking tape and lay the metal strip aside for the moment, remembering to mark which way it should go when fitted.

Cut off the pointed ends of the toothpicks or cocktail sticks and push the cut end into the base or

FIG 14.4 *Window rails*

wall, using a ruler or flat surface to ensure they are the same height before fixing them rigidly in place with a drop of instant glue. Then carefully place the metal strip over the tops of the uprights and secure it with the glue – *see* Fig 14.5.

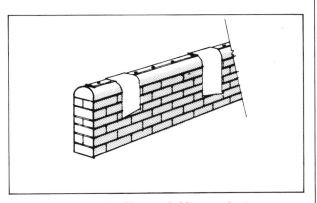

FIG 14.3 *Masking tape holding metal strip*

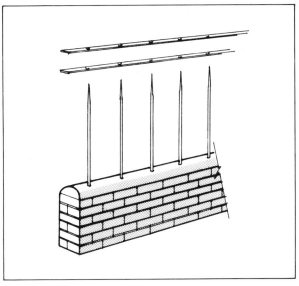

FIG 14.5 *Glue the uprights in place ready for the metal*

To make a right angle joint as shown in Fig 14.6, place one metal strip into position and then place the other strip at right angles before gluing both on to the uprights – the end stick will act as a guide. This same method can be used to good effect for balcony rails, making sure you use a reasonably thick base for the balcony – *see* Fig 14.7.

FIG 14.8 *Railings using nails*

USING NAILS FOR RAILINGS

Various thicknesses and lengths of nails can also be used for making railings – an ordinary-round nail is best. Flat nails can look good, but do not fit as well in the round holes on the metal strip. The flat top of the nail would look quite wrong, so a bit of metal bashing is needed on a shoe last or miniature anvil, as shown in Fig 14.9. A rail made by this method can be seen in the photographs of the two-room house.

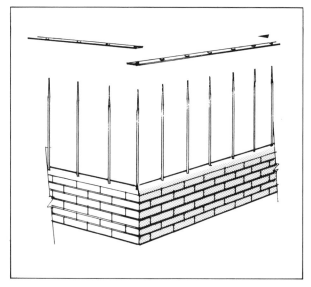

FIG 14.6 *Making a right angle*

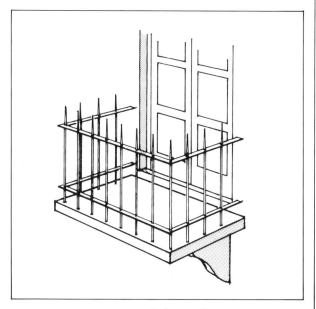

FIG 14.7 *Balcony rails*

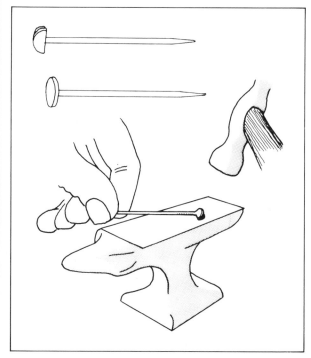

FIG 14.9 *Flattening nails*

CHAPTER FIFTEEN

CHIMNEYS

CHIMNEYS IN THE GEORGIAN and Regency periods differed little from those of the preceding years. The more fanciful Jacobean designs were followed by less exotic ones, but there is still a wide range of variations that can be used by the modeller, and it is worth spending some time on the design and construction to achieve an authentic appearance. Photographs of chimneys on full-sized houses are useful for inspiration, and the following techniques will tell you how to build chimneys successfully.

BRICK FINISHES

The type of chimney most often found on Georgian houses will have a brick finish, and all sorts of decorative variations are possible. For a basic chimney, use either a solid block of wood or ¼″ plywood cut to the shapes shown in Fig 15.2 – if using plywood, the joints should be panel-pinned and glued together. Then, for either method of construction, cut a piece of ¼″ plywood to overlap the top all round by ¼″ and glue and panel-pin this to the top – *see* Fig 15.3.

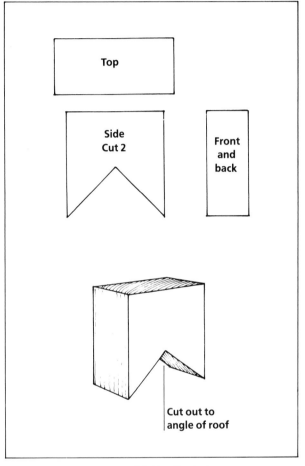

FIG 15.2 *Making the stack*

FIG 15.1 *Weathered chimneys on the town house*

You must now mark out the brick pattern on all four sides of the stack – remember to also mark the corner pieces. For the next stage, the stack must be held firmly (preferably in a vice) while you saw each horizontal line to a depth of ⅛″ with a fine tenon saw or hacksaw. Then very carefully cut the vertical lines marking the brick sizes with a lino or Stanley knife or Exacto tool, making sure not to cut too far and using two cuts to make a V-groove as in

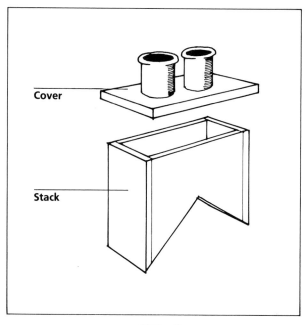

FIG 15.3 *Fitting the cover*

FIG 15.5 *Bricks marked on stack*

Fig 15.4. The finished result should look like that shown in Fig 15.5.

Close study of full-size buildings and of the photographs in the colour section will reveal that old bricks, especially on corners, very rarely keep their squareness – time, wind, rain, wear and tear and careless roofers will have rounded and knocked the corners off, and an authentic model will show this wear.

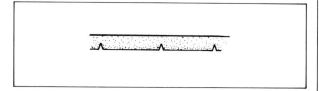

FIG 15.4 *Vertical grooves seen from above*

Using the lino or Stanley knife or Exacto tool, chip and round off the corners of the bricks to produce an effect like the one shown in Fig 15.6. (This illustration features rather more weathering than would usually be found on one stack, but shows the different types of wear.) Do not be

tempted to overdo the weathering – the photographs of the finished models have, we feel, the correct amount.

Make up some Tetrion or plaster and rub it into the grooves – any overspill on to the bricks will provide a nice semi-rough texture. When the plaster or Tetrion is half dry, gently scrape it away

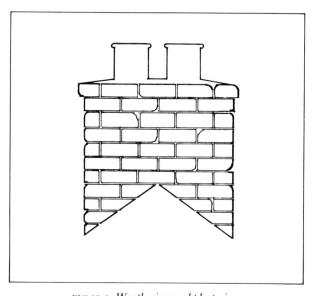

FIG 15.6 *Weathering and plastering*

from the grooves between the bricks with a small screwdriver, remembering to scrape both horizontal and vertical grooves. Fig 15.6 shows the end product – there should be a very thin layer of plaster in each groove, making it slightly hollowed.

When the plaster or Tetrion is completely dry, you can begin painting the bricks. There is a great variety in colour in different areas, from a light buff to a rich red-brown, and once you have chosen your colour, paint it on in matt or water paint, taking great care to avoid getting paint in the grooves. The colour photographs show that the bricks will vary in colour – some will have become dirty and others may have been replaced – let this show in your decoration.

Let the stack dry and turn your attention to the pots, which can be made from a number of materials – ¾″ or 1″ round dowelling or narrow plastic cotton reels are fine. Glue them into place with PVA wood glue as shown in Fig 15.3. An alternative is to use aluminium tube of the same diameter – this, when cut in half with a small hacksaw, can also be used for cowls – *see* Fig 15.7. To get the slight rise at the bottom of the pots, seen in profile in Fig 15.6, spread a 50:50 solution of wood glue and water on the chimney cover and follow this with a thin layer of Tetrion or plaster.

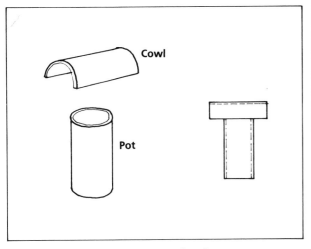

FIG 15.7 *Pot and cowl*

PLASTERED STACKS

Plastered chimney stacks are found on some small country houses and on labourers' cottages, and are simple to make. Use either a solid or built-up construction as shown for Figs 15.2 and 15.3, and instead of marking bricks out, cover the whole chimney with the water and glue size and then with plaster, to achieve a finish shown in Fig 15.8.

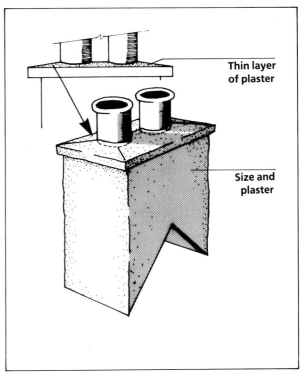

FIG 15.8 *Plaster finish*

FLASHING

Lead or zinc flashing was used in the Georgian era (and still is today) to make a watertight seal where the slates and stack meet at the bottom of the chimney. An authentic model will feature flashing, and it is not difficult to make.

If you decide to add flashing to the chimney stack, this must be done *before painting or plastering the stack*, as the grooves will be used as a guide.

Almost any thin metal is suitable for use, and should be cut as shown in Fig 15.9, to correspond

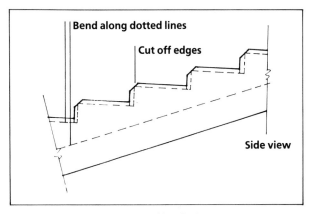

FIG 15.9 *Making flashing*

to the grooves cut in the stack – two or three courses up is usually sufficient. Bend the metal along the dotted lines indicated and glue the flashing into place on the stack with impact adhesive – *see* Fig 15.10 – pressing the bent edges into the grooves. Fig 15.10 also shows how to cut and glue pieces of metal for the front of the stack.

Some older and more remote houses still used cement for flashing, and Fig 15.11 illustrates where to apply a fairly thick mixture of plaster or Tetrion. This should be put on smoothly and carefully and then painted.

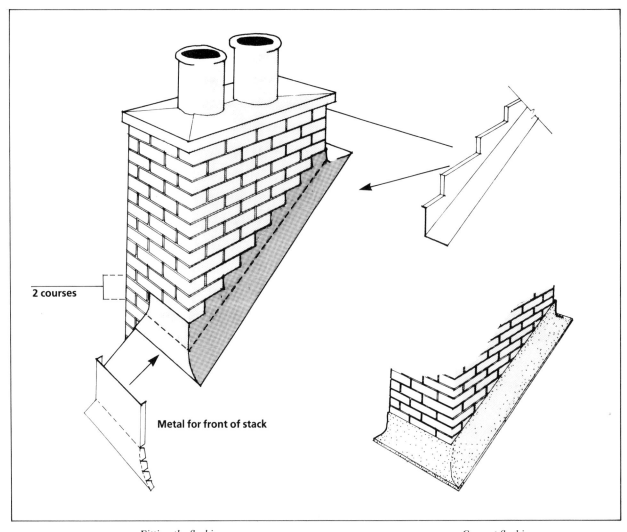

FIG 15.10 *Fitting the flashing*   FIG 15.11 *Cement flashing*

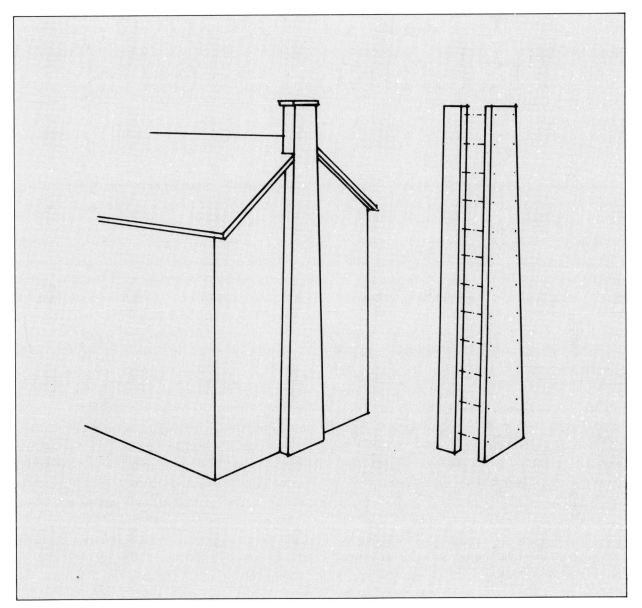

FIG 15.12 *Exterior chimney breast*

EXTERIOR CHIMNEY BREASTS

Exterior chimney breasts are rare on Georgian houses, but are sometimes found on end terrace walls and on houses with the fireplaces on the rear wall – *see* Chapter 2. Either foam or wood can be used – if the latter, cut three pieces from ¼″ softwood and glue and panel-pin them together as shown in Fig 15.12, before gluing the box structure to the side of the house. (Remember to cut a small piece out of the roof panel if you intend to do this!) Foam can simply be cut to the correct size and glued into position. Each method of construction should then be given a brick finish.

CHAPTER SIXTEEN

DECORATION AND FINISHING TOUCHES

INTERIOR DECORATION

Decorating the interior of Georgian houses requires careful attention, not only in the execution but also in the planning. It also requires reference to as much photographic material as can be found – libraries are an excellent source – and the opportunity to explore a full-sized house in your area can prove a perfect mine of information.

Early Georgian houses, particularly country houses, will still have large areas of wood-panelled walls, especially in the larger rooms, as did Jacobean and Stuart houses – I have incorporated this feature into the country house model later in the book. Beams have been included because servants' quarters often retained them – clean-edged rather than adze-marked – and they would often be painted to match the decor. Details are given in Chapter 8.

WALLPAPERS AND COVERINGS

With the advent of new industrial skills craftsmen were able to produce papers for wall coverings, and this became a very stylish and fashionable way to decorate a Georgian house, particularly the town houses belonging to the middle and upper classes and those of rich merchants. Unfortunately it is not really possible to make these highly decorated papers easily yourself, but a number of manufacturers produce excellent copies of Georgian and Regency wallpapers, and there is no shortage of designs. Addresses of the producers of such papers are given at the back of the book.

When choosing your paper, do this with the same care and attention you would use if decorating a full-sized room. The owner of your nearest miniaturist shop will no doubt be pleased to advise you, particularly with co-ordinating papers.

Paint was also used to great effect, and this should likewise be chosen with care. I like to use Humbrol paints (available from most model shops), which come in a wide variety of colours, matt and gloss, in conveniently small cans. Remember to always use an undercoat on surfaces to be painted.

A highly effective alternative to paper is good quality coloured card, available from stationery shops, office suppliers and art shops. It is an excellent way to finish polystyrene foam sheet walls, as can be seen from the photographs of the country house, where the drawing room has been finished in this manner. If cut-outs are made accurately and placed with a piece of contrasting card behind the cut-out, a very fine effect can be obtained – and it is far easier than using contrasting paints.

My daughter and I always completely decorate all panels before final assembly, as this way air bubbles and creases can be eliminated. It is also the only way that skirting boards, picture rails, doors, window frames etc. can be given the finish they deserve – a badly finished wall with runs in it can ruin the appearance of even the best constructed and authentic model.

It is essential to properly match up the pattern of wallpapers, and great care must be taken to ensure that the pattern on one wall is not mismatched by one on an adjoining wall with the pattern upside down. We have all done it in a moment of temporary insanity – so beware!

FIG 16.1 *Three fully-decorated floors*

Sheila and I always use PVA wood adhesive mixed with water in a ratio of one part glue to two parts water – we find this much better than full-size wallpaper glues which can soften the miniature paper unduly and result in rips and tears.

For a successful match at a corner, leave approximately ⅛″ of paper hanging over the edge of one of the walls to be papered, as a butt joint is rarely successful – *see* Fig 16.2 for illustration. When the paper on the one wall is dry, the paper left overhanging should be bent at right angles prior to being glued on the other wall. A very thin coat of glue on the overhanging paper will secure it to the opposing paper neatly and almost invisibly – assuming that the papers have been matched up.

CORNICES AND PATTERNS

Cornices were almost obligatory in Georgian and Regency homes and were often highly embossed, with matching ceiling roses. Again, many different designs are available from specialist miniature producers, but great use can be made of full-sized Anaglypta paper – the patterns must be small and carefully cut to avoid a half pattern ending where it meets the cornice. The ceilings in the Stuart box room and the country house illustrate how this should be done.

Alternatively, suitable pieces of the overall design can be very carefully cut out and stuck on the ceiling in a pattern to match the rest of the room – the interiors of the shop and the large town house show examples of this type of finish. When the sections are securely in place they can be painted with emulsion paint, but you can pick out parts of the pattern in other colours (even gold) if the scheme is to be in the grand manner. Examples of typical Anaglypta patterns can be seen in many photographs in this book.

Cornices can also be made from certain full-size mouldings – Fig 16.4 shows a few examples. The mouldings are available from DIY shops and can be easily cut to the required length. Miniature plaster and wooden mouldings can be obtained from suppliers listed at the back of the book.

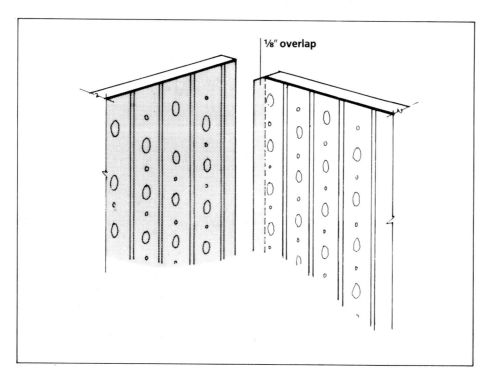

⅛″ overlap

FIG 16.2 *Matching wallpaper at room corners*

FIG 16.3 *Fancy wallpapers*

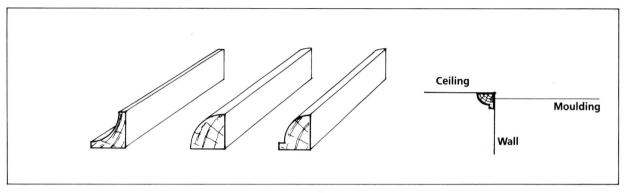

FIG 16.4 *Using mouldings for cornices*

WOOD SURROUNDS

You will notice in the photographs throughout that some decorative panels are surrounded with wood. This is very simple to do. Once the wall has been papered, a further piece of squared or rectangular paper should be cut from a piece in a co-ordinated colour and carefully glued in place. Make sure that it is straight and that if there are to be more than one on a wall, they are equal distances apart. Now cut four pieces of wood (we used commercially-produced miniature picture framing) to the size of the paper panel – ensure that the corners are

FIG 16.5 *Cornices and Anaglypta cut-outs*

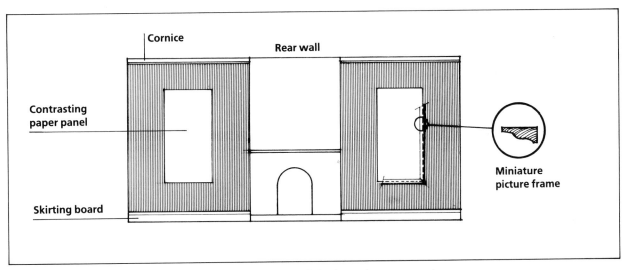

FIG 16.6 *Wood surrounds for decorative paper panels*

FIG 16.7 *Paper panels glued on*

perfectly cut using a mitre, and check that the wood covers the paper panel so that no edges show either inside or outside the wood. Paint the wood frame either to match or contrast with the skirting board, and when dry glue it into position as shown in Fig 16.6.

From the photographs of the shop you will see that decorative panels made from plaster mouldings have been used – the mouldings are available from the same manufacturers as the cornices, ceiling roses, etc. They are difficult to make yourself, but someone skilled at cake decoration may be able to make something similar, using an icing bag and fairly firm plaster. It is worth a try – please let us know if you succeed.

EXTERIOR DECORATION

The various models in this book have been finished in brick, dressed stone, stucco or a mixture of all three. To simulate these finishes is relatively simple but time-consuming and must be tackled with care and attention to detail.

The enthusiast will no doubt have noticed that most model houses for sale at the lower end of the price range are plain colour washed (usually white) – this type of finish is quite acceptable, and can be charming. My daughter and I feel, however, that the warm glow of brick – in many shades, depending on the area – or the elegant appearance of dressed stone can not only impart a solid feeling to the model but also add a pleasant authenticity to the house, and that it is well worth the extra time and effort.

BRICK FINISHES

The method shown in Figs 16.8, 16.9 and 16.11 should first be practiced on a small piece of plywood. The first stage is to paint the plywood with a coat of emulsion paint in a colour to represent the mortar. This will show through, so the mortar colour should be decided early on – we have used white, as this was in common use and really shows the bricks to excellent effect, but black or beige are equally effective and authentic.

Emulsion paint is the best medium to use for brick simulation, but, like the undercoat of white or coloured emulsion, it is water-based and the second coat, which is used for the bricks, may blend

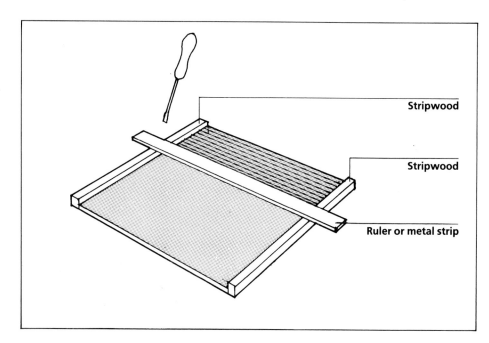

FIG 16.8 *Drawing horizontal lines for bricks*

96

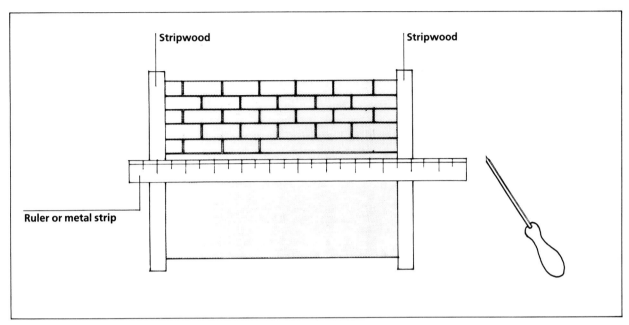

FIG 16.9 *Marking out brick sizes*

into the first coat. It is therefore necessary to insulate the first coat from the second – this can be easily done with a thin coat of matt white (or similar colour to the mortar finish). This type of paint is available from most car shops, usually sold as undercoat. Allow it to dry thoroughly – this does not take long. Alternatively household undercoat, which will dispense with the need for an insulating coat, can be used – it is spirit-based and there will be no possibility of the top coat of emulsion dissolving it.

Next apply a coat of red brick shade emulsion all over the test piece. If you want a rough coat to the bricks, add a sprinkling of sawdust sparingly over the wet paint and then shake off the surplus. Apply another thin coat of red emulsion while it is still wet.

Lay the test piece on a flat surface and place two pieces of stripwood a little thicker than the plywood on either side, as shown in Fig 16.8. Lay a ruler or a flat strip of metal across the test piece, resting it on the pieces of stripwood – the ruler should be no more than ¼" above the plywood.

Using the ruler as a guide, start at one end of the test piece and gently draw a line to the other end with a small screwdriver (*not* a Phillips) with a tip no broader than ³⁄₃₂". The line should be continuous, as stopping and starting does not look good. Move down by the thickness of a brick – ¼" to ¾" for larger bricks – and using the same technique continue to the bottom of the test piece, cleaning the tip of the screwdriver regularly. *See* Fig 16.8.

The next stage is to mark out the brick sizes. Rest your hand on the ruler to steady it and, taking care not to mark over the horizontal lines as this would spoil the whole effect, continue along the row, as shown in Fig 16.9. The next row should be marked below the centre of the first row of bricks. When you are satisfied with your expertise you can confidently transfer this skill to the outside panels of your model.

The same brick finish can also be applied to polystyrene foam sheet walls – give the polystyrene a coat of PVA wood glue diluted with water, one part water to one part glue. Coat smoothly all over

FIG 16.10 *Brick finish and balustrade*

and allow to dry. When dry, mix sufficient Tetrion to make a medium to thick mixture and apply this to the wall with a small artists' spatula or flexible kitchen knife. Put the Tetrion on as smoothly and flat as possible, trying to avoid deep ripples – small runs or ripples can be sanded off with a sanding block when dry – and when thoroughly dry, follow the same procedure as for the plywood application.

DRESSED STONE FINISHES

To produce a dressed stone finish on either plywood or polystyrene sheet, coat the wall with a 50/50 mix of PVA glue and water, allow to dry and then plaster thinly as described above. Before the plaster dries, mark the stones out with a small V-gouge or a screwdriver as shown above. Bear in mind that dressed stone blocks are much bigger than bricks:

FIG 16.11 *Dressed stone marked out*

approximately 1½″ × 1″ is fairly standard on a model house. *See* Fig 16.11 for a detailed illustration. It may be necessary to temporarily nail stripwood to the sides of the model so that the gouge or screwdriver does not touch the panel being worked.

As I have previously said, it *is* demanding work and very time-consuming, but the finished result is extremely rewarding when properly done.

FIG 16.12 *Dressed stone and brick finish*

Do not try to cover too large an area in one go – it is better to paint a panel to a depth of, say, 10″ and then mark out the bricks or stones. The next part can then be carefully painted and marked out. If too large an area is painted, the bottom of the panel may start to dry before you reach it and it will be difficult to mark out the bricks.

The final touch is to apply some odd bricks by varying the colour of the topcoat a little, making some bricks lighter or darker. I also like to spray a very thin coat of matt black over the stone or brick to give a weathered effect. Apply the paint more heavily at the base and thinner up to about 18″ up from the base. In any event, do not overdo it – spray from no closer than three feet from the panel.

RANDOM STONE

Random stone blocks can be seen on many early Georgian country and village houses, and an example of this is shown in Fig 16.13 – if you decide to use this finish, there is no need to smooth the plaster too much, as a rough surface looks better on random stone.

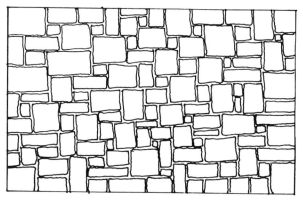

FIG 16.13 *Random stone finish*

In all model building, if an authentic appearance is to be achieved in the final finishing, it is essential that the full-sized subject should be looked at closely and with imagination. For the modeller with some experience, alternative methods will no doubt occur, and these should be experimented with – there are no truly definitive constructional or finishing techniques, and it is all there to explore and interpret artistically.

FINISHING TOUCHES

The finishing touches are the making of all models and can set off your model to perfection. It must always be borne in mind that you are constructing a model house, not a toy. A period house will have much evidence of wear and tear – for instance, roof tiles and slates will show chipping and dis-colouration, and may also have slipped. Both tiles and slates will also have had to be replaced with the passing of time, and some will therefore be of a different appearance, looking newer than the originals.

The roofs will also be stained by droppings, moss stains and the like. The lead flashing around the chimney stack bases will also stain the roof as the lead erodes over the years.

WEATHERING

On a brick finish, try to include a few chipped ones, and some of the corner bricks should be rounded off a little – only new bricks would show a clean edge. Some staining on stucco, stone and brick walls will also be evident under gutterings and around the base of the house. Of course, weathering should not be overdone – close observation of full-sized period houses will show how far you should indicate age on your model.

Do not exclude chimneys and stacks from your observation, as these take a real battering from the elements – chipped and cracked bricks are the rule rather than the exception, and they are more often than not smokestained from a couple of centuries of coal and wood burning.

As can be seen, this is a study in itself and well worth interpreting on your model, as the results will be more than worthwhile and will most certainly be appreciated by the viewer.

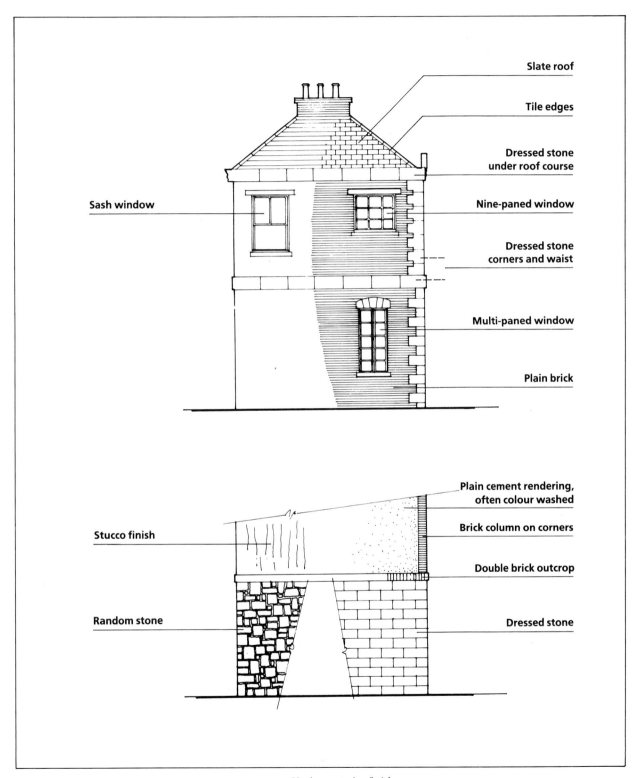

Slate roof

Tile edges

Dressed stone
under roof course

Sash window

Nine-paned window

Dressed stone
corners and waist

Multi-paned window

Plain brick

Plain cement rendering,
often colour washed

Stucco finish

Brick column on corners

Double brick outcrop

Random stone

Dressed stone

FIG 16.14 *Various exterior finishes*

CHAPTER SEVENTEEN

BUILDING A ROOM

UILDING MINIATURE ROOMS can be an absorbing hobby in its own right – first, there is the advantage of the room being quite easy to construct, secondly, it costs little to build and can frequently be constructed from scraps of wood, and thirdly and more importantly, the modeller can concentrate on his or her favourite periods in history or explore the full range of period styles – from Tudor and Jacobean through to Victorian and beyond. The drawings and photographs in this chapter illustrate a few of these styles.

The Stuart room is three-quarter panelled, the ceiling is covered with full-size Anaglypta heavily embossed paper and the mouldings between the panelling and ceiling are cut from the same Anaglypta paper. Such mouldings can be found on the roofs and ceilings of Georgian, Regency and to a lesser extent, Victorian and Edwardian houses and the method of decorating a room or house is dealt with in Chapter 16.

(It should be mentioned that such mouldings are available from various manufacturers – some are

FIG 17.1 *Panelled room with decorative fireplace*

102

actually moulded from real plaster and include cornicing and ceiling roses, while others are made from wood or plastic. See the list at the back of the book for suppliers.)

The Georgian room also makes use of Anaglypta cut-outs, and a trip to your local DIY centre should provide you with a suitable paper. Miniature wallpaper, door surrounds, cornicing and skirting boards are also available from the suppliers listed.

The floor in the Stuart room is produced by the methods shown in Chapter 5, but the floor in the Georgian room is covered by commercially produced planking. This consists of individual planks of wood attached to a strong paper backing which is glued into place, but *not* with a water-based glue.

MAKING A CORNER ROOM

As a first project and as a way of familiarising yourself with the materials, tools and the various finishing techniques covered in the previous chapters, a corner room is an excellent way to gain experience, and a desirable and useful little miniature can be produced at minimal experience.

As with box rooms, if they are all built to a constant size quite a number can be displayed on an average bookshelf. Pieces of furniture can be beautifully shown, and if an opening door is incorporated into the rear wall, a simple box added to that wall could provide the charming addition of a yard or small garden as shown in Fig 17.9, allowing yet more scope for your artistic talents.

The measurements shown in the plans are identical to those shown in the photographs and drawings, but by using the plans as a general guide for layouts a corner room can be made to almost any size.

CONSTRUCTION

The base and roof should be cut to the dimensions shown in Fig 17.2 from ¼" plywood, although ⅜" or even ½" wood can be used – the latter will panel-pin together more easily, but is more expen-

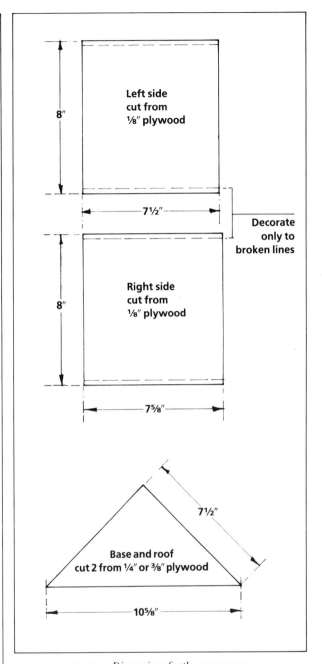

FIG 17.2 *Dimensions for the corner room*

sive – and the two side walls should be cut from ⅛" plywood.

As in all our models, my daughter and I prefer to finish each wall before assembly, and the chapters on finishings, floors, doors, windows etc.

will show you how to do this. Electric lights and illuminated fireplaces add the finishing touch in all model houses and rooms, and instructions are to be found in Chapter 9. The more care you take in the finishing of your corner setting, the prouder you will be of the completed miniature.

Before decorating in your chosen style, mark the top and bottom of both side walls with a pencil to the thickness of the base and roof (*see* Fig 17.2). *Decorate only between these lines.* Now carefully panel-pin and glue the decorated sides to the roof and base as shown in Fig 17.3, noting that the left-hand wall panel is overlapped by the right-hand wall panel at the corner joint.

With the room now complete, it is worth giving some thought to whether to glaze the front – although not essential, it certainly keeps dust out and should be considered. The glazing can be of glass or a clear plastic of Perspex sheet, and it is a simple operation. Cut three pieces of U-channel wood (available from DIY stores), one to the length of the base and the other two to the length of the sides of the room – stain, polish, panel-pin and

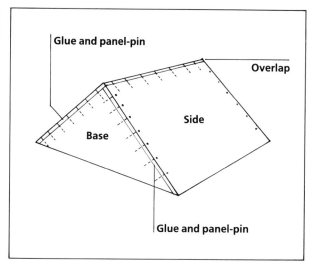

FIG 17.3 *Corner room fitted together*

glue them into place, holding them with masking tape until dry, as seen in Fig 17.4. A piece of glass or Perspex can then be cut to the correct measurements and should slide in and out of the channel without difficulty.

The finishing on the outside of the box is a matter of choice – it can look attractive finished in matt

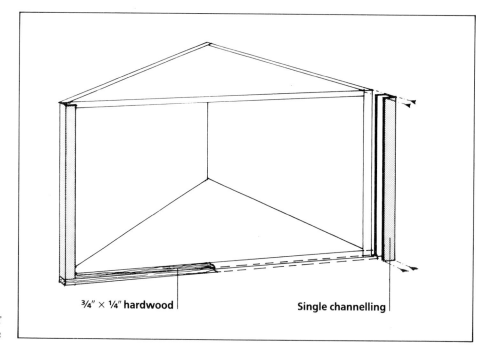

FIG 17.4 *Glazing the corner room*

SINGLE ROOM

The completed room's
impressive fireplace

Oak-stained panels and
white patterns in the room

TWO-ROOM
RECENCY HOUSE

The finished two-room house

Roses (and dressed stone) round the door

Two-room house with one front panel open

*A light and airy
family room*

Finished and furnished

GEORGIAN TOWN HOUSE

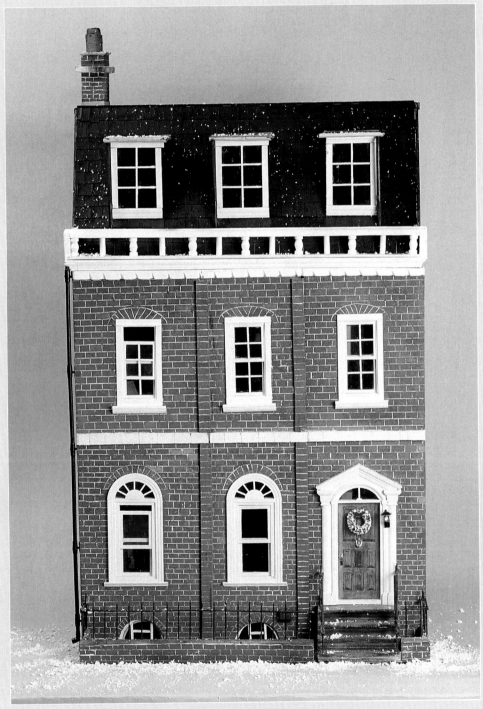

The town house with Christmas wreath and snow

All panels on the town house open

A dramatic use of colour and contrasts

Attic rooms can be plainly decorated

Interior walls with double doors below and single door above

FIG 17.5 *Window, panelling and ceiling*

black, for instance, but my choice is usually to stain and French polish.

To add a back garden or yard without too much additional work, cut four pieces of plywood to the measurements given in Fig 17.6 and panel-pin them together as shown in Fig 17.7. Lay the room

and assembled garden area on a flat surface and glue them together to produce the model seen in Fig 17.8.

Having completed this first project to your satisfaction, you will perhaps now be encouraged to begin work on a full room or one of the houses in this book.

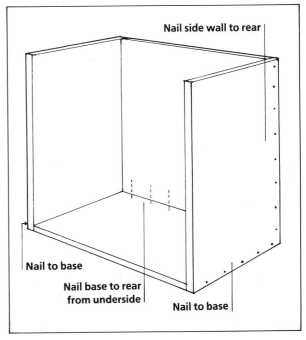

FIG 17.7 *Corner room box fitted together*

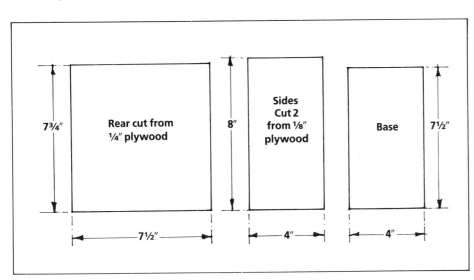

FIG 17.6 *Dimensions for corner room box*

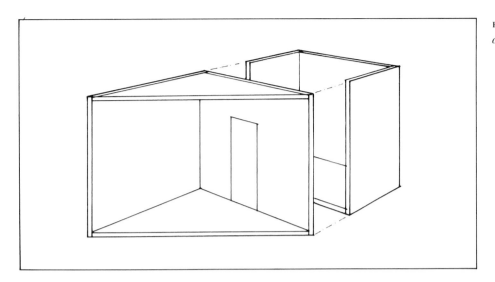

FIG 17.8 *Assembling
corner room and box*

MAKING A ROOM

The base should be cut from ½″ plywood to the measurements shown in Fig 17.10. The roof is cut from the same material, while the side and back panels are best cut from ¼″ plywood.

Assembly is very simple – all that is required is for the side and rear panels to be glued and panel-pinned into position on the sides of the base and roof panel. However, all features such as doors, windows, chimney breasts, panelling etc. should again be added before assembly – and it is impossible to mark out floorboards on the baseboard once the side walls are in position.

CONSTRUCTION

Cut out all the pieces of wood to the dimensions given in Fig 17.10, making sure that if floorboards are to be marked on the base the latter is free from knots or very large grain, as this will ruin the effect. Refer to Chapter 5 for methods of finishing floors.

FIG 17.9 *Box fitted
with garden*

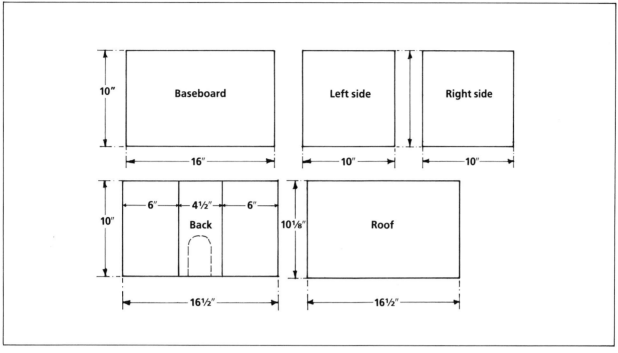

FIG 17.10 *Dimensions for the room*

The roof panel should be decorated next, either with Anaglypta paper or with mouldings – *see* Chapter 16. If you wish to add a ceiling light, this should be done before the roof is papered so that the wiring does not show. However, if you are not papering but using ceiling mouldings, then the wiring can be threaded through a small hole in the ceiling and then run along the top of the exterior of the room box.

The rear wall of the Georgian room features a fireplace, which can be made of wood or of blown polystyrene and should be tackled next – Chapter 9 shows fireplace construction details. Once you have glued the fireplace into place and the glue has dried, the decoration of the walls can begin. (The fire surround shown is a ready-made one, but it is not difficult to make your own out of wood.)

You will see that we have chosen to wallpaper the room and have added decorative wall panels in a co-ordinated colour. The wallpaper can be glued into place with ordinary wallpaper paste or watered-down PVA wood glue. Brush the paste or glue on to the back of the paper as for full-sized paper, and then carefully place it into position and smooth it out with a clean cloth. The paper need not reach the top or bottom of the wall as skirting boards and cornices will be added.

When the paper is dry add the skirting board, which must be carefully mitred at the corners. The next stage is to complete the panels on the rear wall. These are made from picture rail – use the smallest quarter round dowel you can obtain, or buy ready-made panels. The corners must also be mitred precisely. Paint the panels and allow them to dry before cutting two pieces of plain paper to the size of the panels and gluing them on to the rear wall, making sure that they are straight and in the correct position between the fireplace and the side walls. Now glue the wood panelling into place.

When cutting the cornicing, remember to also mitre it carefully so that the joints fit perfectly before gluing it into position.

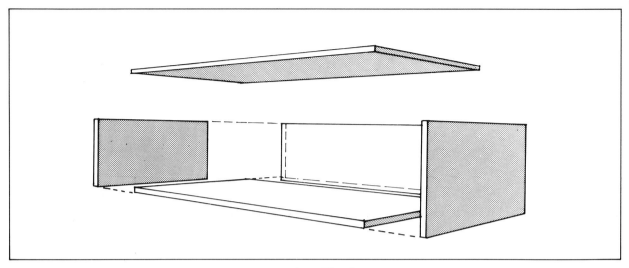

FIG 17.11 *Assembling the room*

When you have finished all the walls, assemble them as shown in Fig 17.11, using glue and panel pins – first glue and nail each side wall into position on the sides of the baseboard. When they are in place, glue and nail the rear wall to the side walls and baseboard, and finally glue and panel-pin the ceiling on to the three walls, each time using masking tape to hold the pieces until the glue sets.

The glazing procedure is identical to that for the corner room – having fitted the three pieces of U-channel wood as shown in Fig 17.12 cut the glass or Perspex to the correct size and gently slide it into place.

To complete your room, either paint or stain and polish the exterior of the box and stand back to admire your achievement.

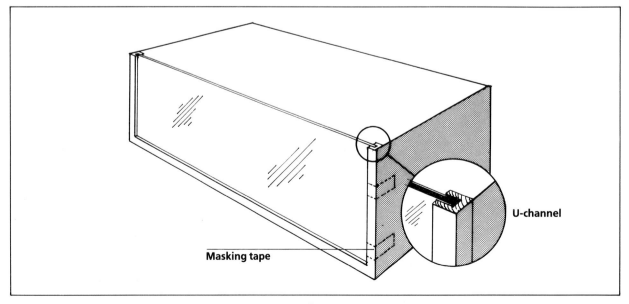

FIG 17.12 *Glazing the room*

CHAPTER EIGHTEEN

TWO-ROOM REGENCY HOUSE

*A*S THIS IS THE FIRST HOUSE PLAN in the book it is a relatively simple two-roomed building, but I have added an entrance hall and landing that could easily accommodate various items of furniture. The model is fairly typical of many Regency houses usually found in terraces, and can be finished either in plain brick, dressed stone or stucco; this model has a dressed stone finish with the lower half brick.

For the construction of this model, we used plywood and 1″ thick high-density polystyrene (available cheaply from most builders' merchants) – two

FIG 18.1 *The two-room house*

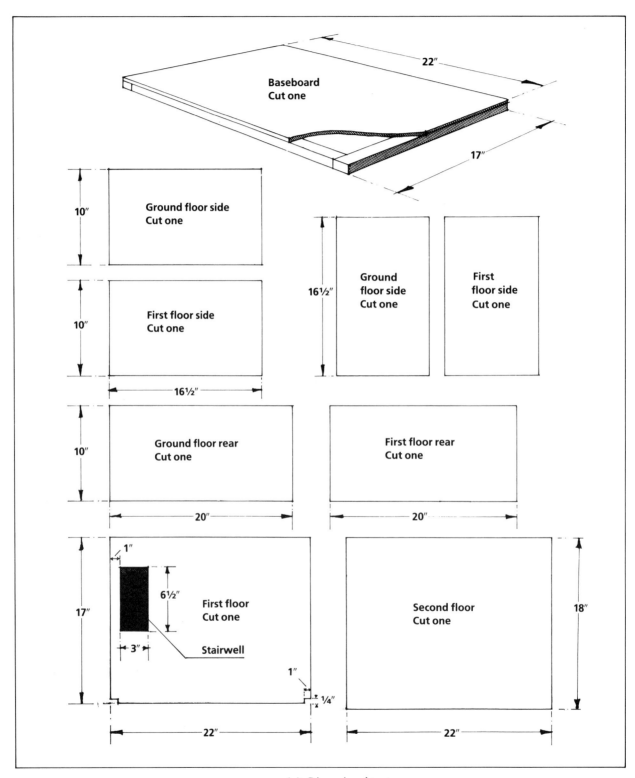

FIG 18.2 (A) *Dimensioned parts*

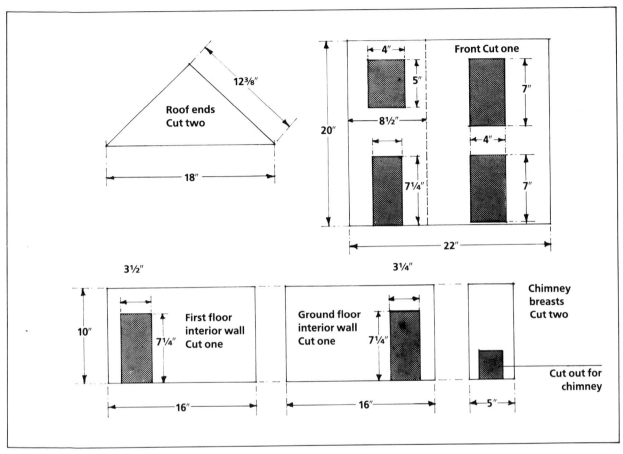

FIG 18.2 (B) *Dimensioned parts*

sheets of 4′ × 2′ should be more than enough for this house. Panel pins are used for the first stage – framing and making the baseboard rigid – and after that only gluing is necessary. Make sure your cutting is accurate and use a set square at every stage to check for squareness and right angles.

The usual practice of my daughter and myself is to finish each internal wall before assembly as we find this the most effective method. (The alternative is to decorate the ground floor before the ceiling is added, though this is more complicated and time-consuming.) Lighting must also be installed before adding the first floor and later the roof. We would always advise lighting a model because, as an unlit room in a full-size house is uninviting, so too is a model room. This also applies to fireplaces, as an

empty grate can look particularly depressing. *See* Chapter 11 for lighting and Chapter 9 for fireplaces.

The windows and doors of this model were commercially produced – if you believe that the construction of the house is within your capabilities but hesitate to attempt the rather intricate work involved in making your own doors and windows, there is a list of stockists and suppliers on page 162. If, however, you wish to produce every item using your own skills, then Chapters 6 and 7 should enable you to succeed.

CONSTRUCTION

Cut a panel of ⅛″ or ¼″ plywood for the baseboard – for ⅛″, the framing should be ¾″ × ½″ woodstrip and the frame should be made up with the ½″ side glued to the underside; for ¼″ plywood, ½″ square framing will suffice. The dimensions of the base and other parts of the model are shown in Fig 18.2.

Glue and panel-pin the frame into place, then mark out the floor as described in Chapter 5 and polish it. Remember not to polish where the polystyrene sheet is to be glued for the side walls, as glue does not take well on a highly-polished or shiny surface.

GROUND FLOOR

The ground floor, side and rear walls must now be cut from the foam sheet to the dimensions given in Fig 18.2. This can be done with a fine-toothed tenon saw or very carefully with a lino knife. Three more identical pieces will be needed later for the upstairs side and rear walls. Cut the chimney breast from the foam sheet for the rear wall with a fretsaw or Stanley knife, and cut out the fireplace opening before gluing the chimney breast in place on the rear wall (refer to Chapter 9 for further information).

With the downstairs openings before you, it is now decision time: do you or do you not decorate first? If you do, *see* Chapter 16 for details; if not, or if you have already decorated, then assembly can begin. Coat the bottom surface of the rear wall with PVA or good quality wood glue and place it accurately at the rear edge of the baseboard, holding it firmly in place to let the glue 'grab'. Now glue the two side walls to the base and back wall in the same way – use a set square to make absolutely sure that all is square. Temporarily hold the walls to the base and each other with masking tape (available from car accessory shops). This is the method for all walls, whether interior or exterior. The two side walls should be positioned ½″ from the front of the base to allow for a wood facing which will later take the hinge for the front of the house (*see* Fig 18.3).

Two pieces of ¼″ plywood are needed for the ceiling of the ground floor (floor of the first floor) and ceiling of the first floor, cut to the dimensions given in Fig 18.2. Cut out the two corner pieces of

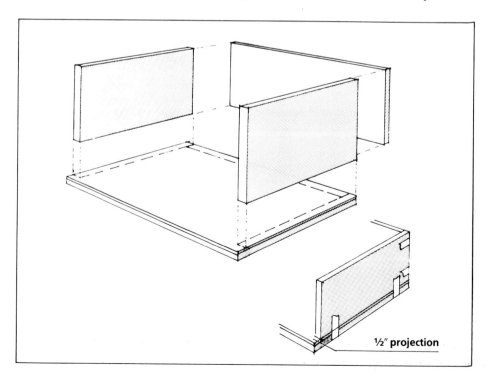

½″ projection

FIG 18.3 *Assembling the ground floor*

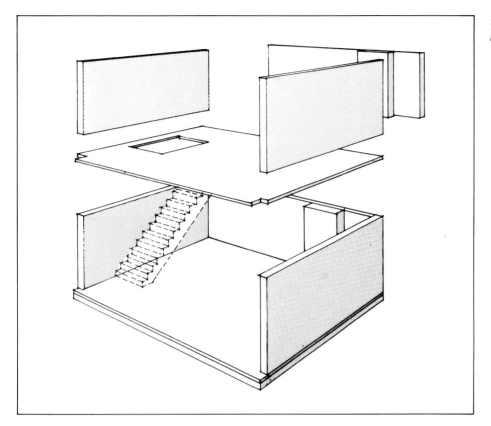

FIG 18.4 *Assembling the first floor*

the ground floor ceiling with a fretsaw or fine-toothed tenon saw, ensuring that you cut out the notches at the front to ½″ deep × 1″ wide as shown, and cut out the stairwell using a fretsaw.

If you intend to fit ceiling lights in your model as recommended, now is the time to do this, particularly as it will enable you to groove the underside of the first floor to take the wiring and then cover the ceiling with the finish of your choice. See Chapter 11 for details of wiring and lighting. We would suggest that the ceiling of the ground floor is also finished before assembly. As the photographs show, we used full-size Anaglypta paper for the ceilings – if you decide to do the same, look for a highly-embossed paper with a suitable small pattern.

The floor/ceiling can now be glued into place and should be held in position with masking tape – weights can be added along the edges until the glue has taken firmly and evenly (*see* Fig 18.4).

FIRST FLOOR

The next stage is to cut out the first floor side and rear walls to the dimensions shown in Fig 18.2 and cut out and glue the chimney breast to the rear opening. This procedure is identical to that for the ground floor, as is the order and method for gluing and taping the first floor walls, as seen in Fig 18.4. Once this has been assembled, the ceiling for the first floor (attic floor) can be marked and cut out, with any grooves and lighting wires installed as before and the ceiling and floor decorated appropriately. When this ceiling is dry it can be glued into place, noting that it overhangs the back by ⅝″ and the front by ⅞″ – when the wood facings for the front walls have been added, this overhang will be reduced to ⅜″ at the front.

With the walls and ceilings now in position, cut the gable ends as shown in Fig 18.2, remembering to cut a notch ¾″ × ¼″ on the rear sides for the

FIG 18.5 *Both floors completed*

ridge beam. Use either foam sheet or ⅛″ plywood for the gables. Glue and tape the gables into place, and when dry glue on the ridge beam, a piece of stripwood 22″ × ¾″ × ¼″, referring to Fig 18.6.

Roof Panels

The roof panels can be cut from ⅛″ plywood or heavy-duty cardboard. The model in the photographs was designed to be part of a terrace, so there is no overhang or any barge boards, and the dimensions given in Fig 18.3 reflect this. (One great advantage of producing your model with plain sides and without an overhanging roof is that this allows you to build a larger model, perhaps the Georgian shop in this book, and simply push the two together to produce part of a terrace or, who knows, in time a terrace of many models.) If you wish to make this model as a detached house, add ½″ to the roof panels on either side; barge boards can be cut from ¾″ × ¼″ whitewood.

Cut out and decorate the roof panels (*see* Chapter 12 for roof decoration) before gluing and taping them to the position indicated in Figs 18.7 and 18.8, remembering to chamfer the top and bottom of each panel – *see* Fig 18.7.

At this stage the essential structure of the model is largely complete, and the chimney stack can be made from either a foam sheet or solid wood (*see* Chapter 15). Glue the chimney on to the roof panel in line with the chimney breasts on the rear walls.

FIG 18.6 *Ends and ridge beam*

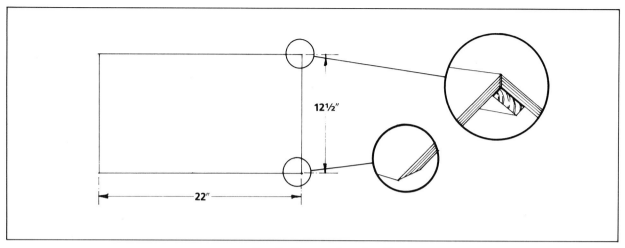

FIG 18.7 *Detail of front roof panel and beam*

INTERIOR WALLS

The two interior dividing walls should now be cut from ⅜″ plywood to the measurements shown in Fig 18.2. Cut out the holes for the interior doors and hang the doors in position. (If you are making your own doors, see Chapter 6: it is by far the most economical and satisfying method.) Add the cornice and skirting boards (*see* Chapter 16) – this helps in fitting the interior walls as it gives an additional surface for gluing them into position. When complete, the walls can be glued and slid carefully into place (*see* Fig 18.10 for position), again using masking tape to hold them until dry.

The staircase should now be accurately glued into the correct position. We have shown in Chapter 10 how to make staircases yourself, but if you wish to save time or feel that making one is beyond your present skill, very good kits are available from various manufacturers, and suppliers' addresses

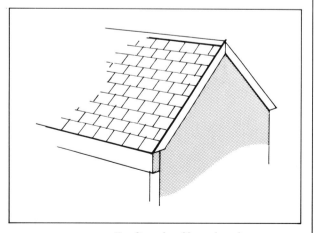

FIG 18.8 *Roof panel and barge board*

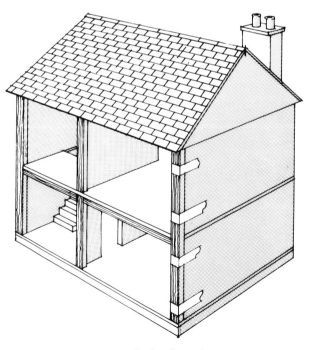

FIG 18.9 *Facing front edges*

116

are given at the back of the book. All the dimensions in the illustrations are for ready-made fittings as well as those made from our designs.

Making and Fitting the Front

Face the front foam edges of the model with ½″ × 1″ strip timber – whitewood is suitable, but make sure you choose knot-free material. This should simply be glued into position as shown in Fig 18.9 and held in place with masking tape until dry. The underside of each ceiling should similarly be framed with ½″ square stripwood as shown in Fig 18.4 – note also that the ceiling framing should of course be placed between the two side facings.

The front of the model is made from ¼″ plywood, and should now be cut to the dimensions given in Fig 18.2, and the door and window openings cut out with a fretsaw. Again, the internal and external decoration should ideally be completed before the door and windows are fixed into place.

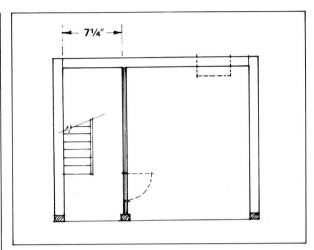

FIG 18.10 *Positioning of walls, doors and chimney breasts*

The model in the photographs is finished in half brick and dressed stone. The red brick shown is ready-made – if you decide to produce your own brickwork, read the instructions in Chapter 16 carefully and practice on small squares of plywood

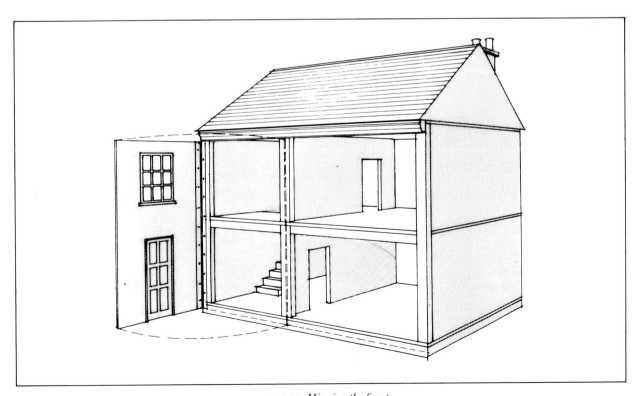

FIG 18.11 *Hinging the front*

before committing yourself to applying the technique to your model. Time and patience will produce results of which you will be proud.

The photographs of this model reveal that there are cornerstones standing proud of the walls. The same stones are used under the fascia and also at the bottom of the front openings; these, together with a vertical and a horizontal column, are the division of the brick and stone work. The stones are cut from balsa or, preferably, whitewood to ⅛″ thick, and are marked out using a shallow V-cut to produce square stones. Again, refer to Chapter 16 for greater detail on finishing techniques.

The completed front openings should now be hinged into position using ½″ or ¾″ piano hinge. A simple method of ensuring that the hinge is in the correct place both on the front and on the wall is to use double-sided tape to hold it to the wood before screwing it frimly into position. The fronts must be placed ¼″ from the top of the side walls and ¾″ from the bottom of the base for ease in opening and closing the model as shown in Fig 18.11. The simplest door fastening, a hook-and-eye catch, can be purchased from any DIY shop.

FINAL TOUCHES

When the openings are in place, add a decorative fascia board above them as shown in Fig 18.6. This board should be at least ½″ thick, enough to cover the openings when closed. (Picture framing of the right width and with an embossed design is ideal.) Carefully glue it into position, holding it with masking tape until dry.

The addition of a front doorstep completes the model – cut it to the same size as the front door (8½″ × 2½″) from a piece of ¾″ or ⅝″ wood and glue it to the underside of the front door panel in the position shown in Fig 18.12, taking great care to avoid gluing it to the bottom of the door. If you really want to add style to your model, then railings (see Chapter 14), wrought iron window guards and one or two door lanterns will finish it off well.

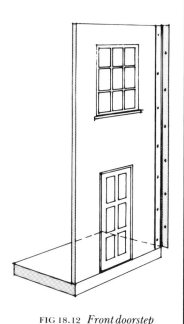

FIG 18.12 *Front doorstep*

FIG 18.13 *Checking the fit of the front*

CHAPTER NINETEEN

GEORGIAN TOWN HOUSE

WHEN DESIGNING THIS MODEL, I decided that it should be the home of a well-to-do family and that the rooms should be large enough to fit quite a few impressive pieces of furniture in. The model is constructed in much the same way as the two-room house, the main difference being that I felt that a basement should be included – it is obviously false, but gives a much grander appearance to the house when combined with the steps up to the rather elegant entrance.

FIG 19.1 *The finished town house*

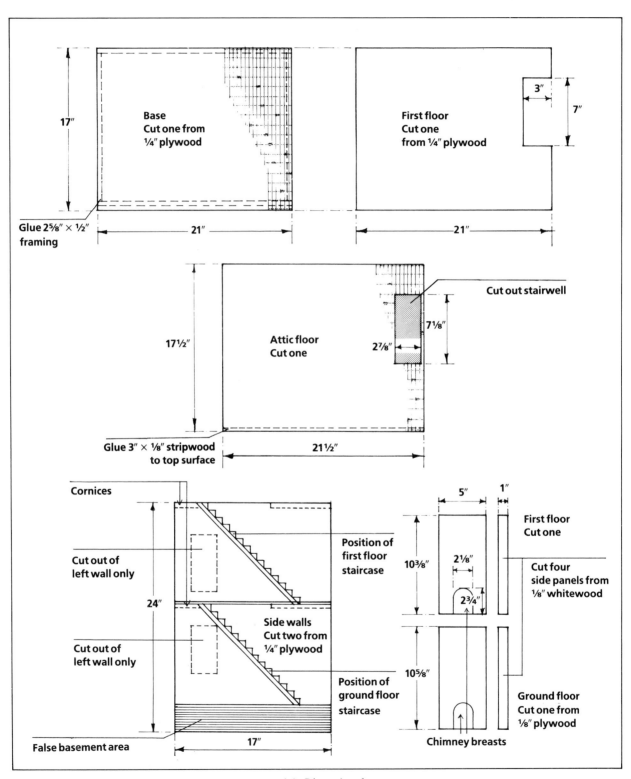

FIG 19.2 (A) *Dimensioned parts*

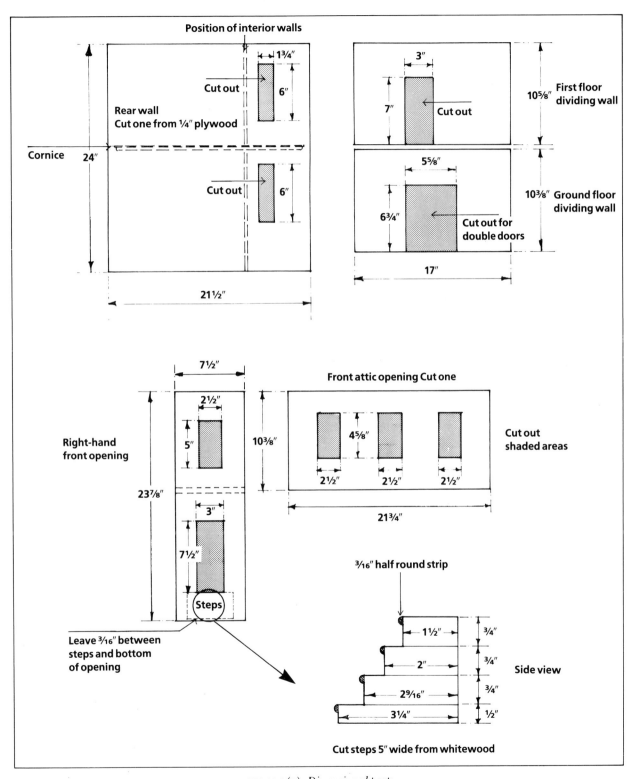

Position of interior walls

1¾"

Cut out

6"

Rear wall
Cut one from ¼" plywood

Cornice

24"

Cut out

6"

21½"

3"

Cut out

7"

10⅝" **First floor dividing wall**

5⅝"

6¾"

Cut out for double doors

10⅜" **Ground floor dividing wall**

17"

7½"

2½"

5"

Right-hand front opening

10⅜"

23⅞"

3"

7½"

Steps

Leave ³⁄₁₆" between steps and bottom of opening

Front attic opening Cut one

4⅝"

Cut out shaded areas

2½"   2½"   2½"

21¾"

³⁄₁₆" **half round strip**

1½"   ¾"

2"   ¾"

2⁹⁄₁₆"   ¾"

3¼"   ½"

Side view

Cut steps 5" wide from whitewood

FIG 19.2 (B) *Dimensioned parts*

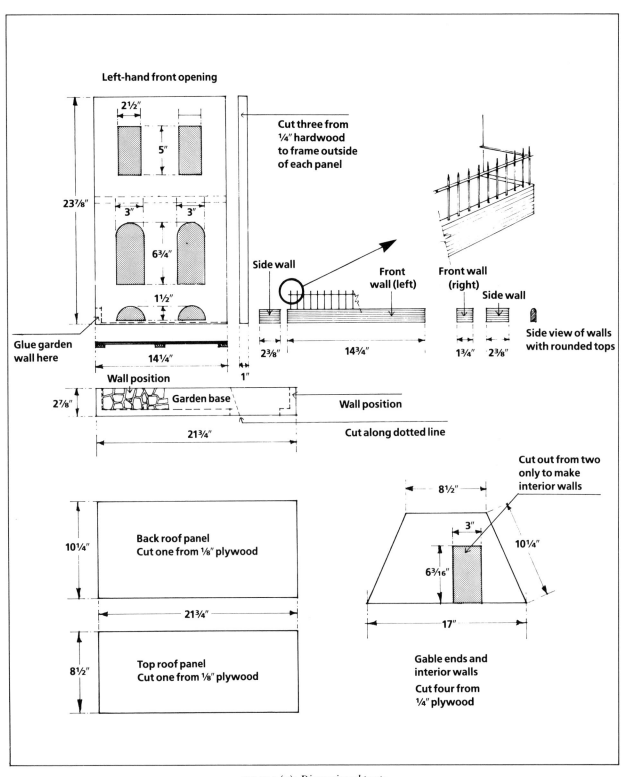

Left-hand front opening

2½"

5"

23⅞"

3" 3"

6¾"

1½"

14¼"

1"

Glue garden wall here

Cut three from ¼" hardwood to frame outside of each panel

Side wall

Front wall (left)

Front wall (right)

Side wall

Side view of walls with rounded tops

2⅜"

14¾"

1¾" 2⅜"

Wall position

2⅞"

Garden base

Wall position

21¾"

Cut along dotted line

Back roof panel
Cut one from ⅛" plywood

10¼"

21¾"

Top roof panel
Cut one from ⅛" plywood

8½"

Cut out from two only to make interior walls

8½"

3"

6³⁄₁₆"

10¼"

17"

Gable ends and interior walls

Cut four from ¼" plywood

FIG 19.2 (C) *Dimensioned parts*

CONSTRUCTION

Cut out all the panels to the measurements shown in Fig 19.2, and if you intend to construct the house in a composite of plywood and polystyrene sheet, allow for the thickness of the foam sheet – 1″ rather than ¼″ plywood. Remember to increase the size of the base by 2″ to allow for the thickness of the foam, and increase the size of both ceilings by 2″. The height of the model will also be greater if you use foam sheet for the walls, as they will be glued on to the top of the base, unlike plywood, which is glued and nailed on to the sides of the base.

A glance at the plans of the two-room house will show you how to construct in foam sheet, but you must face the front of all foam walls with stripwood to allow the hinges for the front openings to be screwed into place.

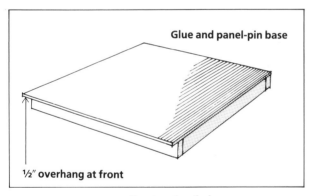

Glue and panel-pin base

½″ overhang at front

FIG 19.3 *Constructing the base*

Begin with the base – build this as shown in Fig 19.3 and finish the flooring as described in Chapter 5. When this is completed and dry, you must decide whether to completely assemble the model and then decorate or (as we do) to finish each panel before assembly. In our opinion, the latter method is the only way that interior decoration can be properly accomplished.

It is also vital to plan in advance every aspect of how you want your finished rooms to look before proceeding any further. For instance, will your house be partially panelled – as shown in the photo-

graphs of the country house – or will it be finished in paper throughout, or papered and painted, or a mixture of all three techniques? All these choices are best decided now, before any further assembly – Chapter 8 has details on panelling, and Chapter 16 on other decoration.

At this stage you should also decide whether you want to install lighting, and if so, whether to fit ceiling lights or wall sconces. And finally, are you going to include a flickering or glowing fire, and with which kind of fire surround? I am sorry to involve you in all this decision-making so early on in the construction, but it is far better to have a clear idea of how you are going to proceed before it is too late to change.

Chapter 16 covers virtually all aspects of interior decoration. Tastes vary enormously of course, but I hope that the photographs of the finished models will inspire you. A study of full-sized Georgian and Regency rooms is also a satisfying source of inspiration.

WALLS AND FLOORS

Assuming that all interior decoration has been finished, the side walls should be glued and panel-pinned into the correct position. When everything is dry, the rear wall can now be similarly glued and panel-pinned into place. Glue the cornices into

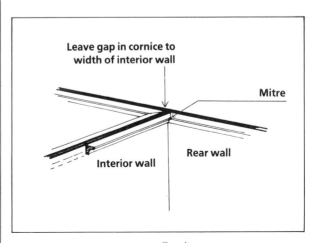

Leave gap in cornice to width of interior wall

Mitre

Rear wall

Interior wall

FIG 19.4 *Cornices*

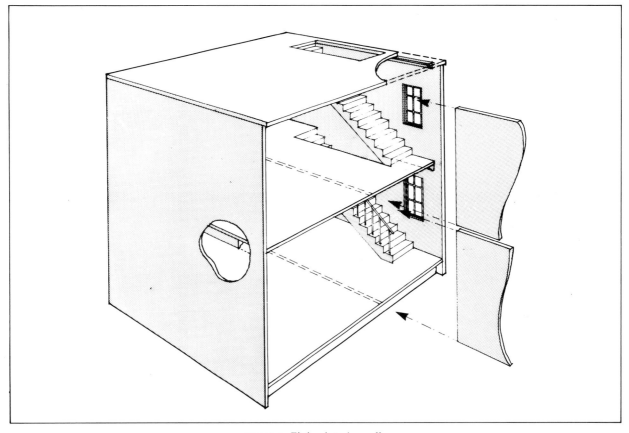

FIG 19.5 *Fitting interior walls*

position, noting the gap left in the rear wall for the interior walls (*see* Fig 19.4) – this should make the walls match up perfectly, and once the cornices are dry and firm, the first floor/ceiling can be glued on, using weights to hold it on to the cornices until dry – heavy books are ideal for this purpose. The same procedure is used to glue the second floor/ceiling into position.

The staircases and interior walls should now be fitted. The staircases shown in this model are commercial kits, which save a lot of time, if time is of the essence. Alternatively, *see* Chapter 10 for all the information you will need to make your own – they are not difficult to build, but must be constructed with care and attention to detail. Similarly, commercially-made doors are incorporated in this model, but these are easy to make – *see* Chapter 6.

When the staircases have been glued in place and have dried, carefully slide and glue the interior walls into position, as shown in Fig 19.5, remembering to mitre and match the cornices (*see* Fig 19.4).

FRONT OPENINGS

It is now time to turn your attention to the front openings, cutting out the door and window openings with a fretsaw. Again, commercially-produced windows were used in this model, but Chapter 7 gives construction details. Obviously, if cost is not a factor, commercial units reduce the building time, but to produce your own is certainly very satisfying and is surely the aim of a true craftsman.

Paint the doors and windows before assembly – as previously stated, this will be very difficult to do once the internal walls are in place. This done, now you must decide what finish you wish to use for the fronts. I chose brick all over with a prominent column of bricks to hide the piano hinges and openings, as shown in the photographs, but a dress stone finish or a mixture of the two can be applied, as can be seen on the shop. For details on these finishings, refer to Chapter 16.

FRONT AREA AND FINISHING

On this model there is also a small brick-enclosed area attached to both front openings. Fig 19.2 shows the measurements and types of wood used in the construction, and railings can be added – I think they provide a very authentic touch. They are easily made from strip metal and toothpicks – *see* Chapter 14.

This front area must be cut into two pieces, as illustrated in Fig 19.2, to enable the fronts to close snugly. The base is made from plywood, and when completed should be glued to the bottom of each front – *see* Fig 19.6. The front door steps should also be glued into position on the smaller front opening and front area.

Before hinging the completed front openings into place, glue ½″ square stripwood to the underside of each floor/ceiling and down the inside front

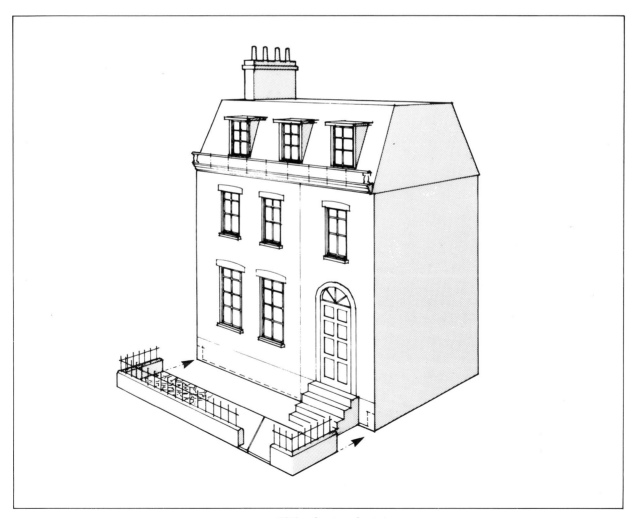

FIG 19.6 *Fitting front garden to house*

FIG 19.7 *Front garden and steps in place*

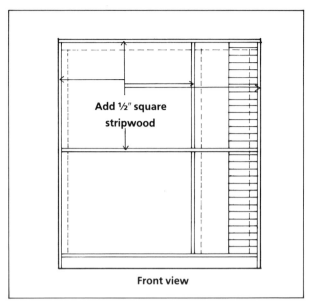

Add ½" square stripwood

Front view

FIG 19.8 *Framing the front*

of both side wall panels – *see* Fig 19.8. These side strips are essential for securely screwing the piano hinges.

Take great care to ensure that the front opening panels are perfectly placed so that the fronts close together accurately. To help position the hinges, I find double-sided tape indispensable – when placed where the hinge is to go, it will hold the weight of the front. This method has the added advantage that if you have fitted the front incorrectly it can be removed and repositioned, and once in the desired position the front openings can be screwed into place. The joint can then be hidden with a raised brick pillow or stone-finished column.

The two side walls can now be finished in the same style as the fronts, and the rear wall can also be finished once all the electrical outlets have been tidied up – it is quite acceptable to finish this wall in stucco, though you may want to continue a brick finish all round. All the electric cables in my models

are stuck down with masking tape and the whole area is then covered by a coat of Tetrion. When this has dried, I finish it with a coat of white emulsion paint.

ATTIC AND ROOF

Now glue and nail the roof panels into place – the two side roof panels should be fitted before panel-pinning and gluing the top and then the rear roof panels. The finished interior attic walls can then be slid and glued into place, and then glue ½" square stripwood along the underside of the top roof panel front, as shown in Fig 19.9. When it is secure and dry, carefully plane the stripwood to the correct angle to take the front roof panel hinge and allow that panel to close.

Having glued the attic windows to the front roof panel (*see* Fig 19.10), the whole assembly should now be screwed into position. For simplicity, screw one face of the piano hinge directly on to the roof top, as illustrated in Figs 19.11 and 19.12, and then screw the front roof panel to the other hinge face. You can then glue a piece of black card over the piano hinge to mask it.

FIG 19.9 *Assembling and framing the roof*

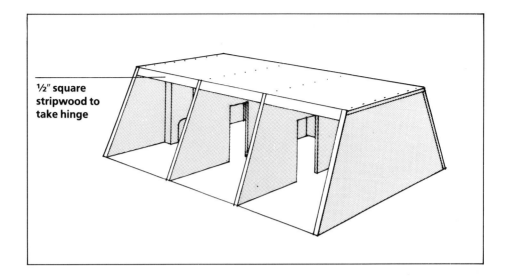

½" square
stripwood to
take hinge

FIG 19.10 *Attic dormer windows*

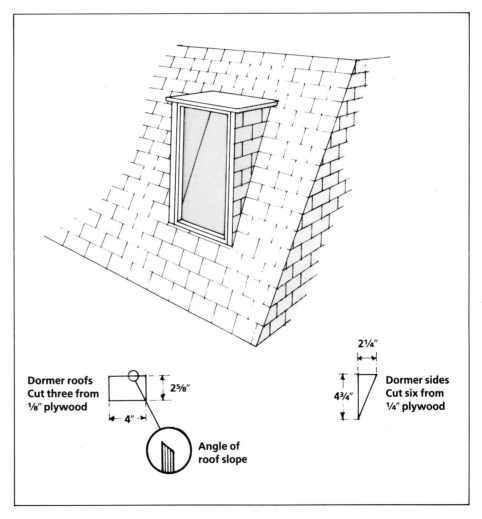

Dormer roofs
Cut three from
⅛" plywood

2⅝"

4"

Angle of
roof slope

2¼"

4¾"

Dormer sides
Cut six from
¼" plywood

BALUSTRADE AND CHIMNEYS

As the photographs and Figs 19.13 and 19.14 show, the balustrade fitted to the bottom of the front roof panel is made up of stripwood sections with ⅜" hardwood dowel and ¾" balsa dowel. The hardwood dowel is left plain and used for every other rail, and the hand-carved balsa dowel is used for the rest of the rails – the balustrade should be glued to a piece of ½" × ⅛" stripwood planed to the angle of the roof. You should also add a chimney – the different styles are shown in Chapter 15, and the one used in the photographs is to be seen in Fig 19.15.

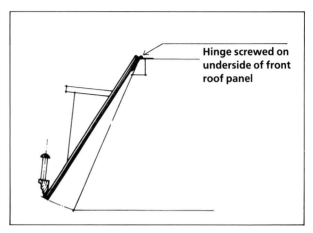

Hinge screwed on underside of front roof panel

FIG 19.11 *Roof hinge*

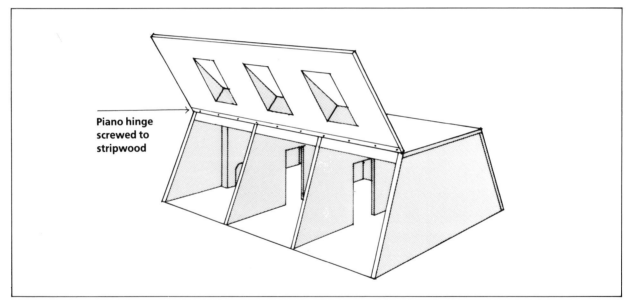

Piano hinge screwed to stripwood

FIG 19.12 *Front roof panel in place*

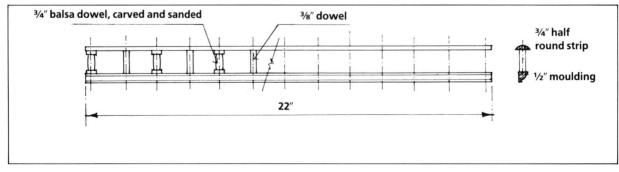

¾" balsa dowel, carved and sanded

⅜" dowel

¾" half round strip

½" moulding

22"

FIG 19.13 *Constructing a balustrade*

I would now sit back and take a breather before attending to the downspouts and realistic slating for the roof. All the relevant information for these will be found in Chapters 12 and 13.

On contemplating the house, I think you will agree that an impressive model has been created which will bring enjoyment to you and to others for many years to come.

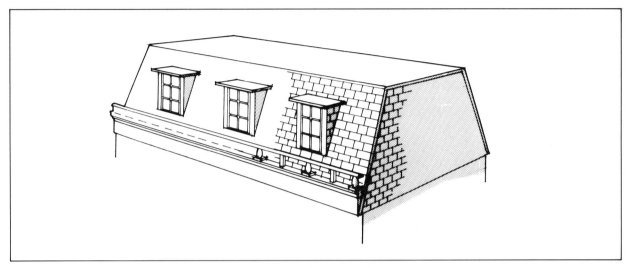

FIG 19.14 *Balustrade in place*

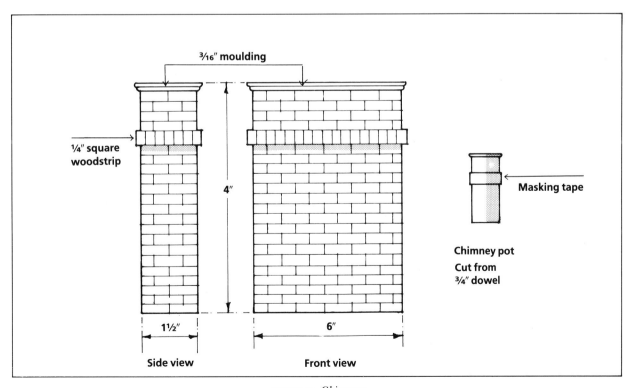

³⁄₁₆″ moulding

¼″ square woodstrip

4″

Masking tape

Chimney pot
Cut from
¾″ dowel

1½″

6″

Side view

Front view

FIG 19.15 *Chimneys*

CHAPTER TWENTY

THREE-ROOM GEORGIAN SHOP

MY DAUGHTER DESIGNED THIS MODEL and decided that it should have a large selling area to be used for any one of several purposes – we have shown it as an antiques shop, but it could easily be used as a tea shop, or any other shop for that matter. The rooms above the shop are large enough for most types of furnishings, and the outside has been finished in dressed stone on the ground floor with bricks providing a contrast on the upper floors. The model is basically constructed in the same way as the two-roomed house and the town house.

FIG 20.1 *The Georgian shop*

FIG 20.2 *Front view*

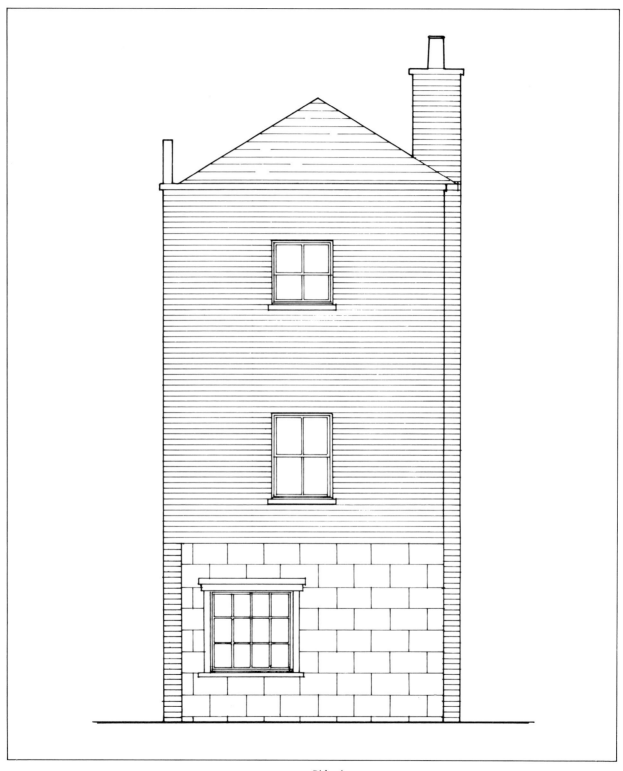

FIG 20.3 *Side view*

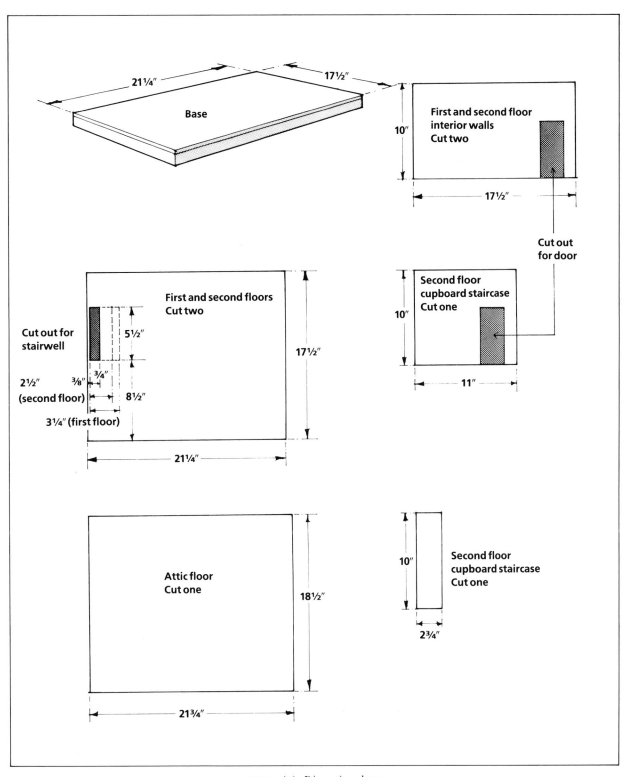

FIG 20.4 (A) *Dimensioned parts*

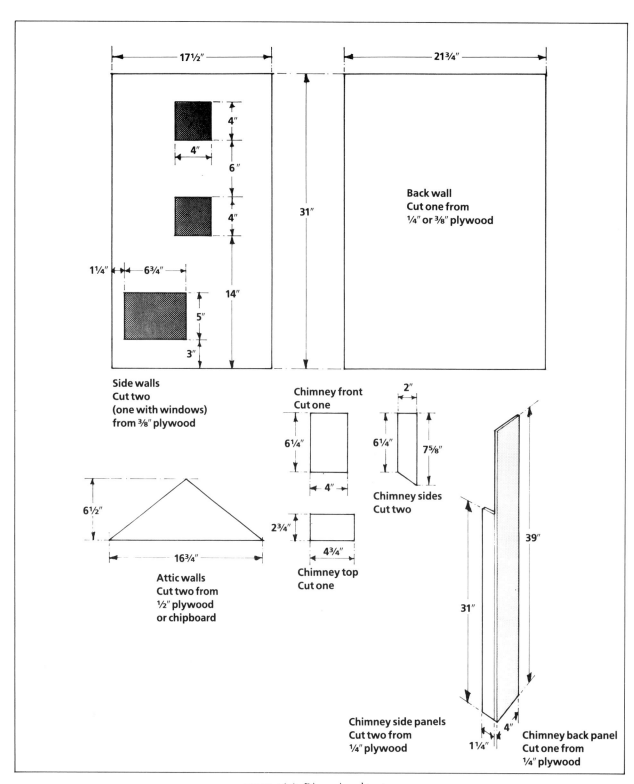

FIG 20.4 (B) *Dimensioned parts*

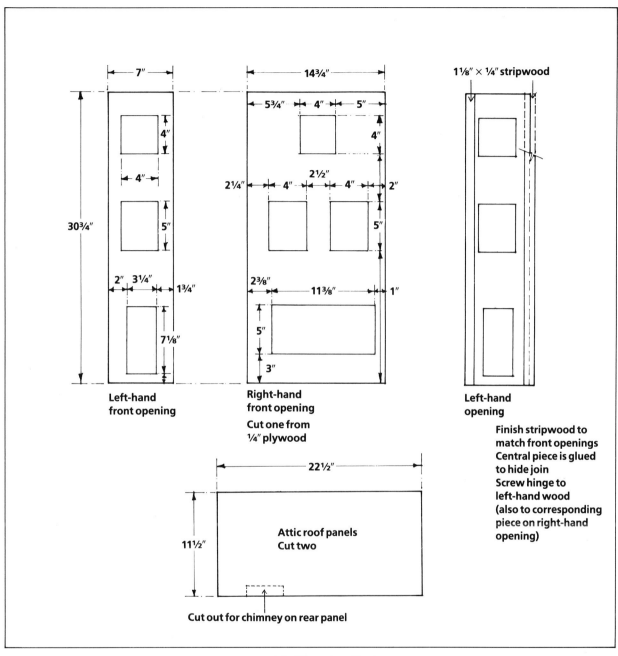

FIG 20.4 (C) *Dimensioned parts*

CONSTRUCTION

Cut all the panels to the measurements given in the plans in Fig 20.4. These measurements are for an all-plywood construction, but a composite of plywood and polystyrene foam sheet can be used if allowance is made for the different thicknesses of the materials (*see* Chapter 19). Also remember that if you use polystyrene, the front edges must be faced with woodstrip so that the front openings can be hinged on to a stable and firm surface.

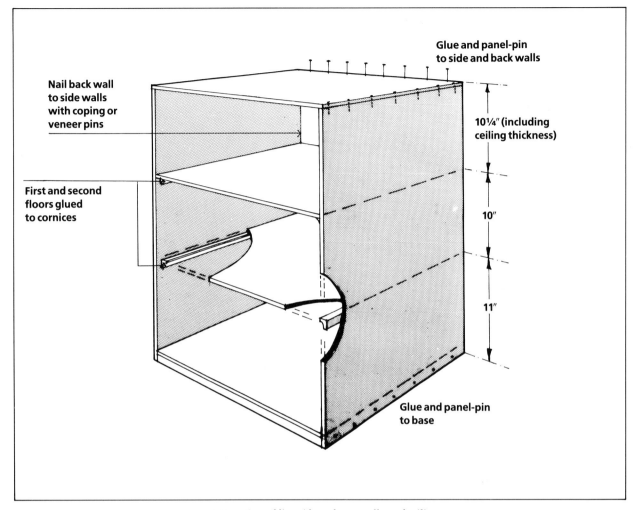

FIG 20.5 *Assembling side and rear walls and ceilings*

As with all the models, begin with the base. We used ¼" plywood framed with ¾" × ½" stripwood. 1" plywood can be used if preferred, but this is not only very heavy but also expensive. Finish the flooring either with commercially-produced planking or in the manner described in Chapter 5.

It is now time to decide on the decor, as decoration should be carried out before the model is assembled – this is not essential, but does make matters much easier in the long run. Great care must be taken to ensure that wallpaper patterns, cornices and skirting boards match up perfectly when the walls are glued and panel-pinned in place.

You will see from the plans in Fig 20.5 that all the floors/ceilings are glued to the ceiling cornices – this gives a strong joint and is very effective. Note that the cornice on the top floor should be glued to the very top of the side and rear walls to support the final ceiling.

All the rooms in this model have been wallpapered. Some have contrasting panels and others are papered with one paper on the lower part on the wall and another above the dado rail, as can be seen in the photographs.

It will also be necessary at this stage to decide on lighting. Is the model to be electrically lit, and if so,

FIG 20.6 *View through side window*

where are the lights to be placed? It will be essential to make provision for any ceiling and wall lights together with wall plugs. Are you planning to include electric flickering or glowing fires? You will have to find room for the cable. If you intend to use one of the commercially-available flickering fire units, refer to Chapters 9 and 11, as a hollow chimney breast will be needed to take in the flickering unit, and the outer chimney will have to be hollow to take the wiring.

WALLS AND CEILINGS

When you have finished all the interior decorating, glue and panel-pin the side walls into place as shown in Fig 20.5, and allow them to dry before gluing and panel-pinning the rear wall carefully into position.

As long as the cornices and skirting boards have been accurately glued into place and they match up perfectly, you can then glue the ceilings/floors into position – after decoration, of course. Use weights to hold them in place until dry. The final ceiling is slightly larger than the others, as can be seen from the measurements in Fig 20.4 – this is because it is to be glued and panel-pinned on to the side and rear walls to make a rigid box (*see* Fig 20.5).

Now glue the two staircases into position – the one on the ground floor is a commercially-produced kit that is easy to construct, and the one on the first floor is made as shown in Chapter 10 and is also simple to build.

The decorated interior walls, with doors fitted, should now be glued in place, ensuring that they are in the correct position and that all cornices, skirting boards and paper match up.

FRONT OPENINGS

With the interior completed, you can now turn your attention to the two front openings. Cut out the door and window openings with a fretsaw and check that the stained or painted door and windows

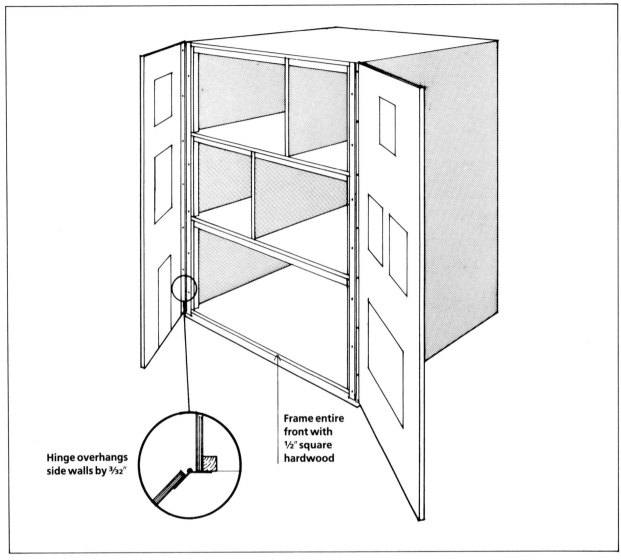

FIG 20.7 *Hinging the fronts*

Hinge overhangs
side walls by ³⁄₃₂″

Frame entire
front with
½″ square
hardwood

will fit. Those in this model are commercially produced, and the shop window has been slightly altered to fit the design, but instructions on building your own doors and windows are given in Chapters 6 and 7.

Chapter 16 covers all exterior stone and brick detail, and this should be completed before the door and windows are glued into place. You will see from the photographs of this model that prominent brick columns have been added to hide the piano

hinge and the joint where the front opens. The two rear side columns are made from ⅞″ triangular section and are finished in stone at the bottom and brick at the top.

Before the front openings are hinged in place, glue ½″ square stripwood to the the underside of each floor/ceiling and down the inside of both front side panels. The wood down the sides is essential for the piano hinge to be securely screwed into place. *See* Fig 20.7.

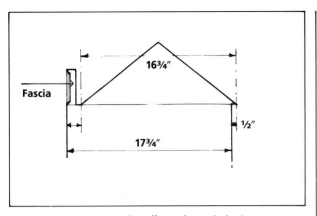

FIG 20.8 *Attic walls overhang the back*

The front openings should be positioned with care so that they can close together accurately – position the hinge so that it overlaps the side walls by ³⁄₃₂″ to allow full movement of the front opening. Double-sided tape is a great help when holding the hinge in position before screwing it into place. The joint is then hidden with the brick column mentioned above.

Finish the two side walls in the same style as the front openings before turning your attention to the rear wall, first tidying up the electric wires and gluing the rear chimney into place. The rear wall can either be finished in the same style as the front and sides or it can be given a layer of Tetrion to form a stucco finish, as described in Chapter 16.

ATTIC, ROOF AND FASCIA

The two side attic walls can now be glued into place – note that they should be 1½″ from the front to allow for the fascia, and will therefore overhang at the back by ½″, as shown in Fig 20.8. Glue a roof beam of 19¾″ × ½″ square between the apexes to ensure that they are in the right position – *see* Fig 20.9.

When the attic side walls and beam are dry, the front fascia, made from ¾″ or 1″ chipboard to the dimensions shown in Fig 20.10 and decorated with architrave or other moulding (Fig 20.11), can be glued into place. Finish the attic side walls in the same style as the main side walls.

It is essential to slate the front roof panel before gluing it into position, as the front fascia may be in

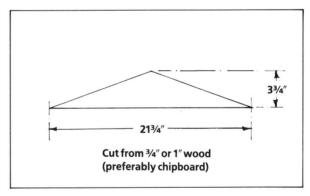

FIG 20.10 *Fascia dimensions*

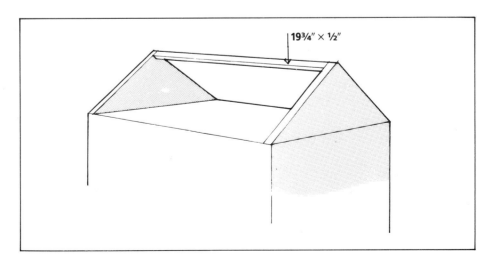

FIG 20.9 *Fitting roof beam*

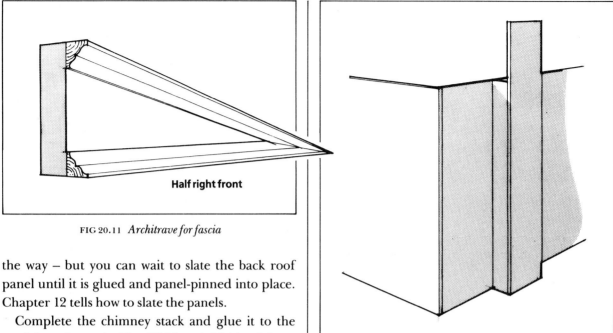

Half right front

FIG 20.11 *Architrave for fascia*

FIG 20.12 *Fitting chimney to rear wall*

the way – but you can wait to slate the back roof panel until it is glued and panel-pinned into place. Chapter 12 tells how to slate the panels.

Complete the chimney stack and glue it to the model as shown in Figs 20.12 and 20.14 – I have given the dimensions of the stack used in our model, but any of the various designs described in Chapter 15 can be used – finish by adding pots and cowling as required. The model is virtually complete, and to add a true scale feel to it add the downspouts and guttering, which are featured in detail in Chapter 13. A look at how to apply the

finishing touches in Chapter 16 should bring the true seal of authenticity to the shop.

I think that you will find that all your efforts have been rewarded and that this large model will bring you many years of enjoyment.

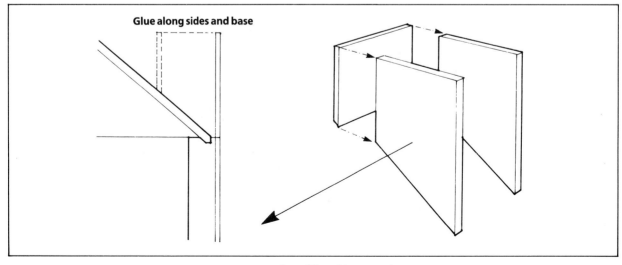

Glue along sides and base

FIG 20.13 *Assembling chimney stack*

FIG 20.14 *The completed shop, fully furnished*

141

CHAPTER TWENTY-ONE

SIX-ROOM COUNTRY HOUSE

FIG 21.1 *The completed country house*

*I*N DESIGNING THIS COUNTRY HOUSE I intentionally moved back to the time of the first George to avoid producing that now rather stereotyped later Georgian house made by toy manufacturers.

Georgian houses, built from warm brick and with dressed stone embellishments, have a charm all of their own, and their wood-panelled interior walls and ornate ceilings still retain much of the cosy glow of the Tudor and Stuart periods. This model represents a typical small manor house.

Whilst the model requires care – dare we say loving care – in the building, we are sure that you will find the final results well worth your time and effort. The plans clearly show the structure of the house, and the photographs illustrate how we have treated the interior and exterior of the finished model. The builder may have his or her own ideas as to how they wish the finished model to look, and with this in mind we hope that the chapters on chimneys, doors, windows and fittings will enable you to succeed in this aim. Again, staircase construction is not shown on the plans – Chapter 10 gives instructions on making your own, or commercial staircases can be purchased and used.

CONSTRUCTION

As with the other models in this book, the country house is built from a combination of plywood and foam. The base is made of ¼″ plywood, as are the

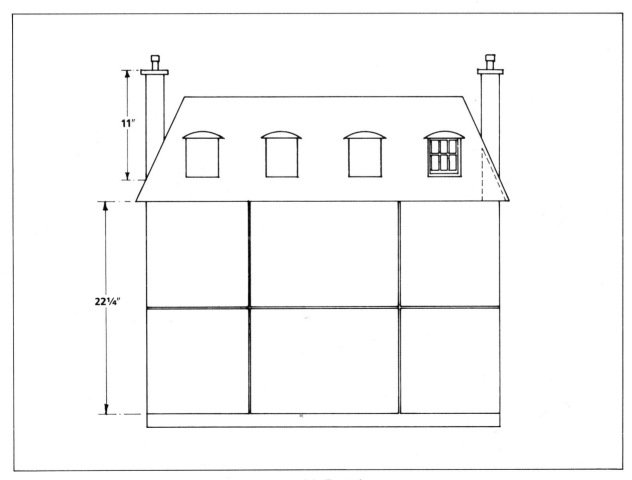

FIG 21.2 (A) *Front view*

143

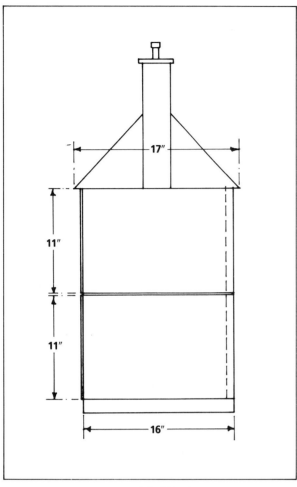

FIG 21.2 (B) *Side view*

ground and first floor ceilings, the fronts and the dividing walls throughout. The sides and back are made of 1″ medium-density polystyrene, and the roof and side panels are cut from ⅛″ plywood. Make sure you cut out the various pieces accurately.

Cut out the base to 17″ × 38″ and frame the underside with 1″ square hardwood or whitewood by tacking and gluing as shown in Fig 21.3. Mark out the floorboards as described in Chapter 5 – it is worth spending time on this, as the result is very rewarding. (Floorboarding in ready-to-lay sheets is quite satisfactory if time is short and expense not a consideration.) When staining and putting the final polish on the floor, mark out carefully the positions of the exterior and interior walls (shown shaded in Fig 21.4) so that you will glue the foam and wood to bare wood.

WALLS

Cut the side and rear walls from the polystyrene foam, using a power bandsaw (if available) or a lino or Exacto knife (which give a smoother finish). (Wood can be used for the walls, but for ease and speed in building we recommend the foam sheet, as in this form of construction nails can be avoided without loss of strength.) The ground and first floors each have two side walls and one rear wall

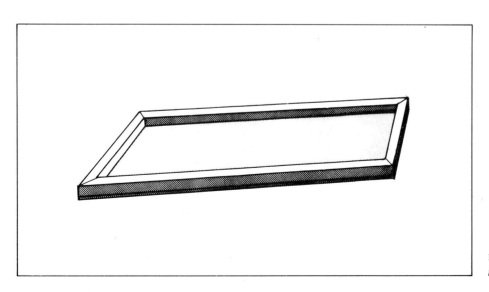

FIG 21.3 *Framing the baseboard*

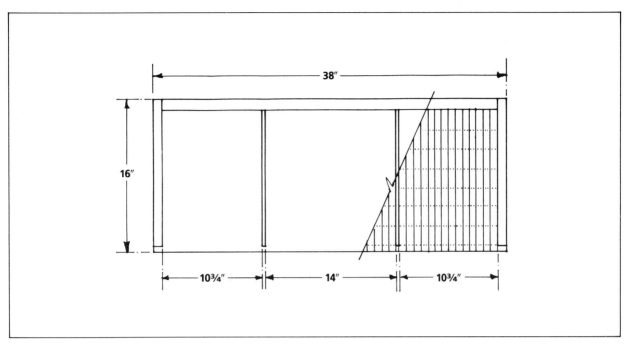

FIG 21.4 *Marking out wall positions on the floor*

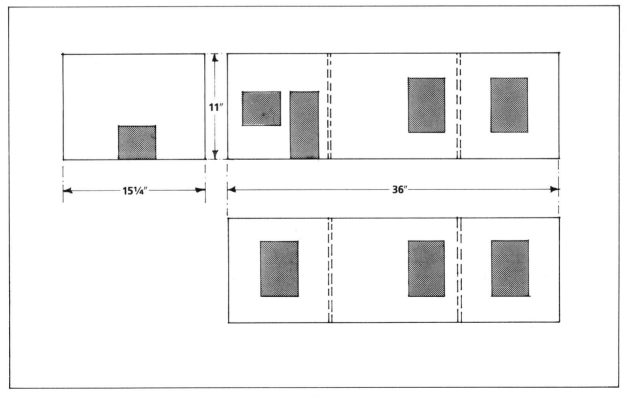

FIG 21.5 (A) *Dimensioned parts*

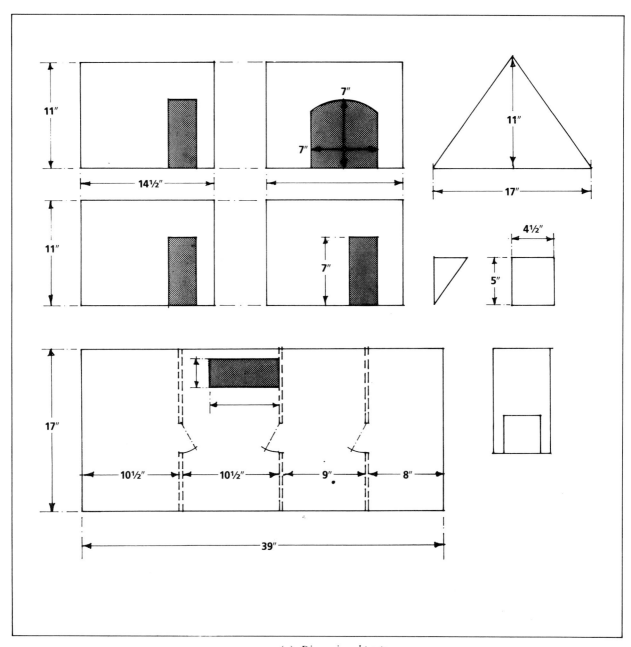

FIG 21.5 (B) *Dimensioned parts*

and two interior walls, while the attic has three interior walls. All dimensions are shown in Fig 21.5.

When you have cut out the interior walls, also cut out all the window and door openings for the ground floor before assembly. We find it a good idea to install the windows at this point, and if you plan to make your own, turn to Chapters 6 and 7. (Commercially-made doors and windows can be ordered from the stockists at the back of the book.)

If you plan to illuminate the fireplace, now is the time to cut out the openings in the side walls, as this will provide all the room needed for lighting.

146

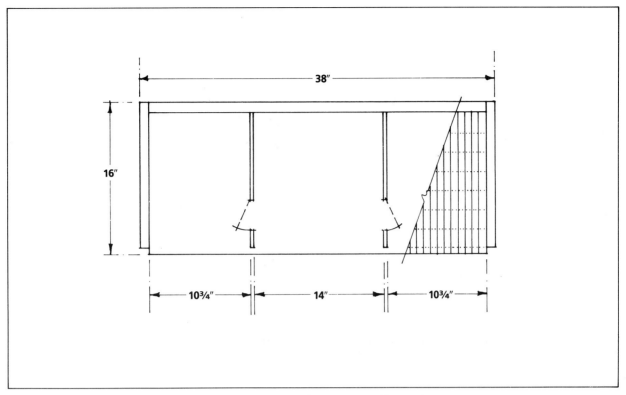

FIG 21.6 *Positioning of interior ground floor walls*

Cut all the way through the foam sheet as for the windows and doors, as the opening can easily be covered with cardboard or 1mm plywood before the external finish is added – *see* Chapters 9 and 11 for making and lighting fireplaces.

Now glue the lower side and rear walls into position, starting as before with the rear wall (*see* Chapter 18). When the glue has begun to 'grab', glue and place the side walls in position, using masking tape to keep them square. Remove the tape when the joints are dry – Fig 21.8 shows the walls in position.

As mentioned earlier, my daughter and I always finish all the interior walls before assembly. Therefore, we would always complete the interior/dividing walls, hang the doors (Fig 21.5 gives you the choice of fitting double or single doors according to preference) and add the chimney breasts – it is also wise to install the electric wiring at this stage,

assuming that the model is to be lit. Fig 21.6 shows the dimensions and positioning of the interior ground floor walls, which should be carefully glued and taped to the unfinished strips of the base floor. The staircase can now be glued to the interior and rear walls and to the floor.

CEILINGS

When all the downstairs walls are in place and fully dry, the masking tape can be removed and the ground floor ceiling/first storey floor added. Remember to cut out the stairwell to the correct size and in the appropriate place before scribing the floorboard sheets. It is a good idea to finish the ceiling side now, as it will be difficult to decorate effectively once it is in position. (*See* Chapters 5 and 16).

Glue the floor/ceiling into place and put weights evenly along the top edges to maintain contact with

FIG 21.7 *Completed bedroom*

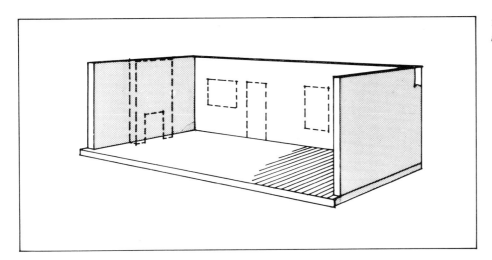

FIG 21.8 *Assembling the ground floor*

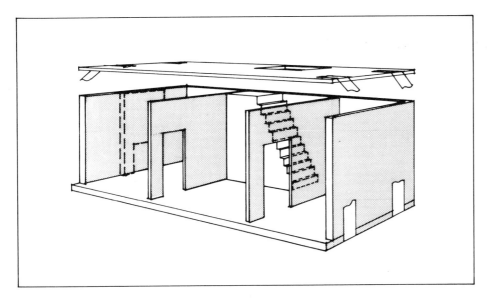

FIG 21.9 *Adding the ground floor ceiling*

the walls until the joints have dried. Masking tape will also help keep everything in position as shown in Fig 21.9.

All the first floor components should be cut out to the measurements shown in Figs 21.2, 21.4 and 21.5. Assembling the first floor is virtually identical to the procedure for the ground floor – decorate all the walls before assembly and install the chimney breasts and any wiring and lighting. Glue the rear and side walls into place, and when dry add the interior walls and staircase as for the ground floor.

ATTIC WALLS

The attic floor/first floor ceiling should now be cut out to the correct dimensions and the stairwell cut out. This floor is larger than the base or the first storey floor, to allow for a ½″ overhang all around the model (see Fig 21.10) – make sure that the overhang is equal all round before using glue, masking tape and weights to make an even contact. This finishes the construction of the first floor.

Refer to Fig 21.5 for the internal walls and to Fig 21.11 for the measurements of the attic side walls and position of the windows and measurements of

FIG 21.10 *Assembling the first floor and ceiling*

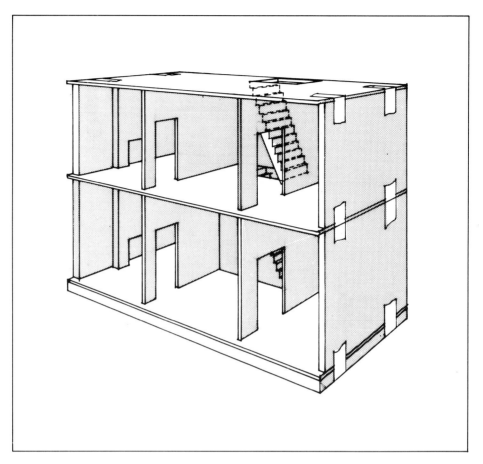

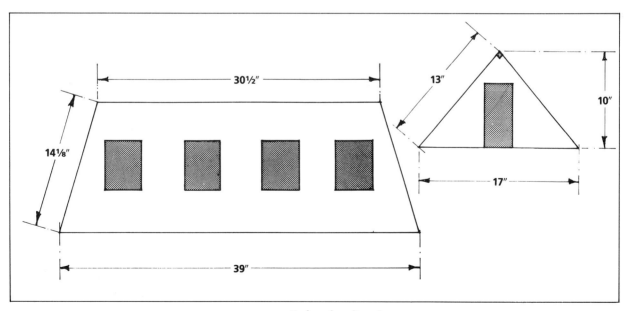

FIG 21.11 *Ends and roof panels*

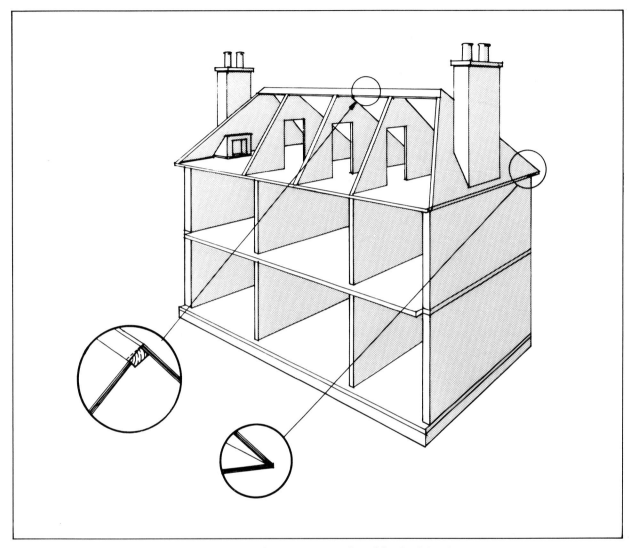

FIG 21.12 *Fitting the interior attic walls and details of chamfer*

the roof panels. When cutting the side panels, remember to cut a notch of ¾″ × ⅜″ for the roof beam – the same notch should also be cut from the three internal attic walls when you cut out the door openings.

When you have completed all the attic interior walls by decorating and fitting the doors (see the appropriate chapters), the two side walls can be glued into place. This is a rather tricky operation, and great care must be taken to make sure that both are placed at the correct angle. Prop the walls

in position with paint cans or similar reasonably heavy objects, and glue the roof beam (30″ × ¾″ × ⅜″ stripwood) in position – this will help obtain the correct angle. When the glue alone is holding the side panels in place, but is not completely dry, glue and tape the rear roof panel in place, having first carefully chamfered the lower edge to fit accurately on to the attic floor (see Fig 21.12).

When all is completely dry and solid, the finished interior walls can be glued into their positions and held with tape until dry. Because of the angle

151

FIG 21.13 *Framing the front*

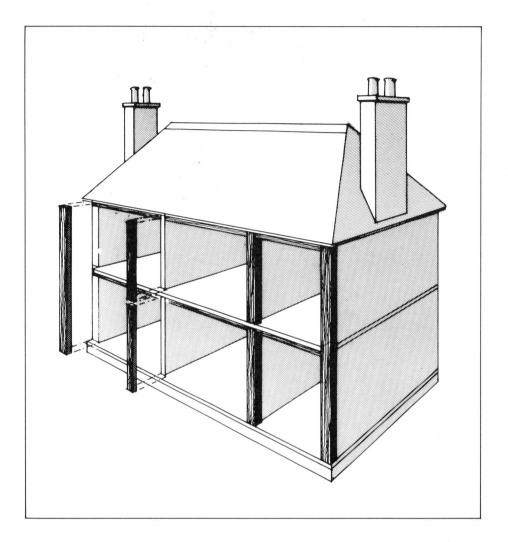

of the attic walls, the roof beam will need planing carefully to the exact angle of the walls as shown in Fig 21.12, so that when the front roof panel is hinged in place it will close perfectly.

FRAMING THE FRONT

Frame the underside of the ground and first floor ceilings with ¼″ square hardwood, using PVA wood glue. The fronts of the four dividing interior walls should also be faced with ¾″ × ½″ strips, gluing the ½″ side to the walls. Cut one long piece of ¾″ × 1″ whitewood or similar wood for each side wall and glue and tape this into place, gluing the ½″ side to the wall and keeping the outside

edge flush (see Fig 21.13). This will have the effect of greatly strengthening your model and making it more rigid. All these strips can now be painted.

DORMER WINDOWS

The four dormer window openings should have been cut out of the front roof panel when you cut it to size (the dimensions are given in Fig 21.11) – paint or decorate the underside and install the dormer window units. The dimensions for the dormer roofs and sides are shown in Fig 21.5, and you can either make your own windows, as shown in Chapter 7, or buy them ready-made. Glue and tape each side panel into position and while they

THREE-ROOM GEORGIAN SHOP

The completed shop

*The shop interior
– complete . . .*

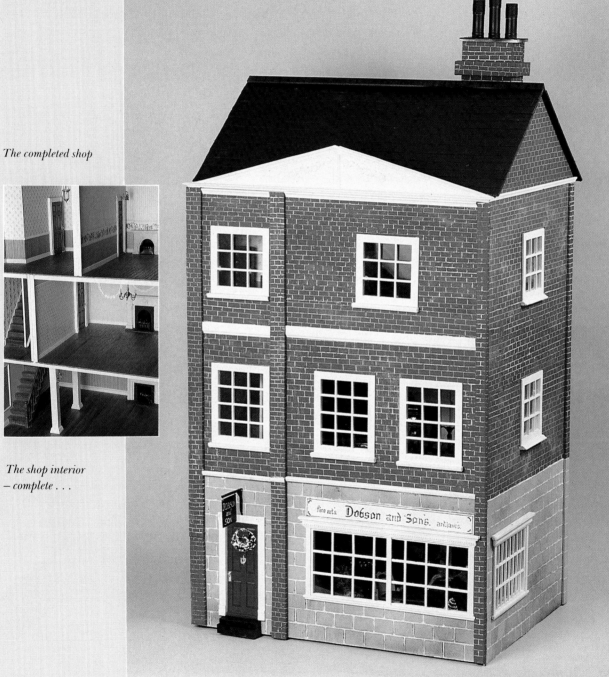

. . . and furnished

Antiques shop ground floor

*Wall lights and a frieze
in a child's room*

*Note the Anaglypta
cut-outs on the ceiling*

*Contrasting paper
panels and an
elegant fireplace*

SIX-ROOM
COUNTRY HOUSE

The country house

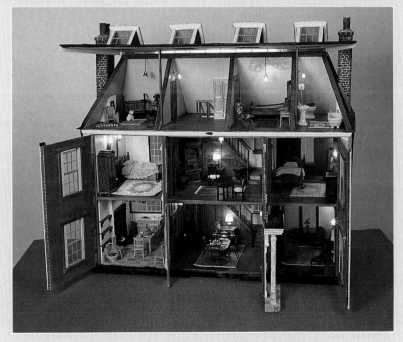

All panels open and all lighting on

The study, complete with panelling and decorative staircase

Oak-panelled country house dining room

The kitchen includes the range and beams

Attic bedroom and bathroom

FIG 21.14 *The kitchen*

are drying, chamfer the rear of the roof panel to fit the angle of the main roof, as illustrated in Fig 21.15. Glue the dormer roof to the sides and add the windows.

You now have a choice of finish for the dormer roofs – you can leave them flat or you can round them by cutting 8 pieces of ¼" or ½" balsa or strip-wood to the shape shown in Fig 21.16. Glue one to the front of each dormer roof and chamfer and glue one to the rear. Use either stiff card or thin aluminium to give a rounded top, and finish as suggested in Chapter 12.

ROOF AND CHIMNEYS

When the front panel is thus completed, it can now be screwed into place. This tricky job can be made easier by the use of double-sided tape. Cut the piano hinge to size and simply tape one side to the correct position on the roof panel – the tape will hold it very firmly, and it can then be screwed into position. Repeat this procedure, taping the hinge on to the roof beam and carefully screwing the hinge to the beam.

The chimney stacks should now be cut from 2" × 3" solid wood to the bottom of the attic floor. Cut once along the angle of the roof side panel and glue the top piece to the top of the panel, having

FIG 21.16 *Finishing the dormer roof*

lined it up with the chimney breasts on the ground and first floors. The lower piece can then be glued on to the attic floor in line with the chimney breasts and stack.

It is time now to stand back and admire the work that you have completed. At this stage the model should look very much like a true model house, particularly if you have decorated and electrified it as you have gone along.

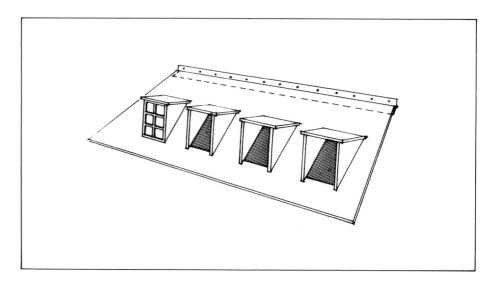

FIG 21.15 *Dormer windows*

154

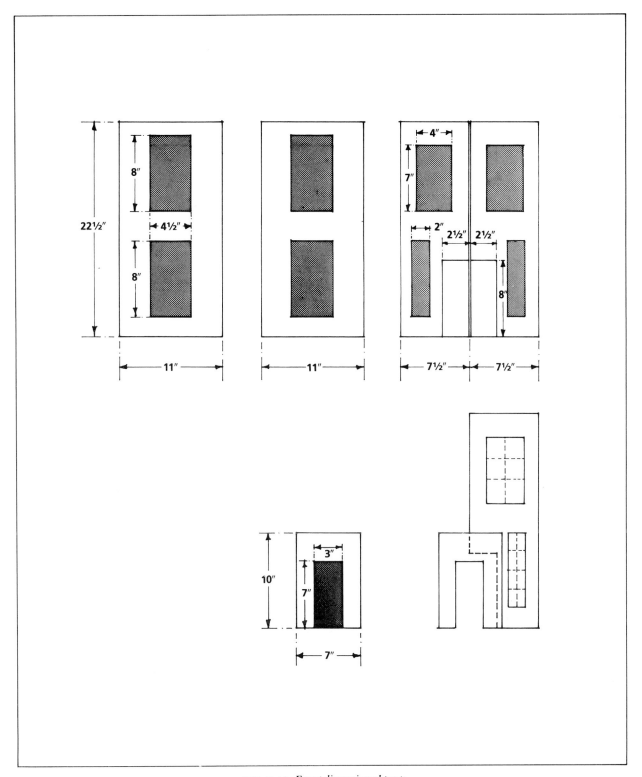

FIG. 21.17 *Front dimensioned parts*

FRONT PANELS

The front of the house is made from four panels of ¼″ plywood – the dimensions are given in Fig 21.17. Cut out the window and door openings carefully, either to the sizes shown if you plan to make your own doors and windows or to the dimensions of ready-made ones.

Consideration should now be given to how you wish to finish your model. Chapter 16, which shows how to put on brick, dressed stone, random stone (still to be seen on many Georgian houses, especially country houses), plain cement or plaster rendering (stucco) finishes, should give you some ideas. The photographs of our model reveal a brick finish with dressed stone corners and side walls – we believe that this finish gives a warm appearance, one that Jane Austen would have felt at home in – as always, however, the final choice is yours.

Whatever that choice may be, we would advise that, as with the interior, all four front openings should be finished before final assembly – but do not fit the windows until the decoration has been completed.

The left and right front openings should now be hinged in place to the outside wall facings. Again, we would suggest that the piano hinges are fixed into position using double-sided tape. This will allow you to position the openings with confidence and accuracy before inserting and tightening the screws. It is important to leave ¼″ space between the fronts and the roof edge to allow room for the guttering, which should be made up according to the instructions in Chapter 13. Also make sure that the fronts only extend to the middle of the base edge (about ⅜″ in) to permit easy opening (see Fig 21.18).

With the two side openings in the correct position and closing snugly on the front of the model, you can now turn your attention to the two middle openings, starting with the assembly of the porch. This is fairly intricate, as can be seen from the illustrations in Figs 21.20 and 21.21, and care must be taken in assembly.

First cut a piece of ¼″ plywood to the measurements shown in Fig 21.19 (10″ × 7″) and cut out the door opening with a fretsaw. A suitable front door must now be made, possibly from the cut-out piece if you have been precise, or from a ¼″ piece of plywood (it can be purchased to fit exactly). Hinge the door into position.

Plain wood (¼″ × ³⁄₁₆″ stripwood is ideal) or suitable moulding should now be cut for the door surround and glued into place, followed by the semicircular decorative stonework above the door shown in Fig 21.19. This is cut from ¼″ whitewood or balsa wood, and the grooves are made with a lino or Stanley knife before the piece is painted and glued.

PORCH

Now cut the porch roof – balsa wood (7″ × ¾″ × 1½″) is quite strong enough, and a piece of moulding will be required for the front (see Fig 21.20). (Picture framing is excellent for this, but other suitable mouldings are available from DIY shops and miniature manufacturers.) Cut the moulding to size and mitre the front corners very carefully before gluing them into position. Now glue the porch roof in place, using masking tape to hold it until the glue has begun to set. Next cut a piece of ½″ thick whitewood or balsa wood to the same measurements as the porch roof and glue this into position at the base of the door opening, ensuring that the front door can move freely.

The two porch pillars can now be cut from ½″ dowel. When you have smoothed off the ends, wrap 1″ masking tape firmly around the top and bottom of each pillar to ⅙″ depth and then repeat this process with ½″ masking tape, as illustrated in Fig 21.20. Coat the tape with PVA glue to round off the sharp corners before giving the pillars a marbled or stone finish. They should be glued at the front corners of the porch between the roof and base, and a piece of 7″ × 2½″ balsa or whitewood should be added, of a sufficient thickness to make up the

156

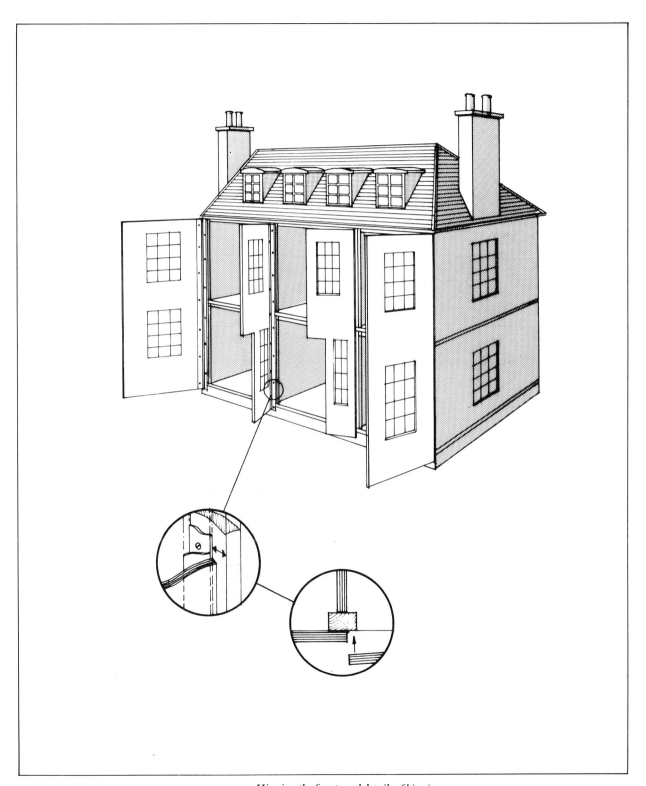

FIG 21.18 *Hinging the fronts and details of hinging*

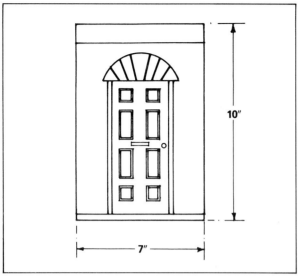

FIG 21.19 *Front door and surround*

gap between the bottom of the porch and the surface the model will rest on. Make sure that there is space for the front panel to move freely.

With the porch complete and appropriately finished, it is time to glue the whole assembly on to the front of the right central opening (*see* Fig 21.21) – this must be done very precisely and accurately to allow the front door to move freely into the house when the front openings are closed. Take great care with this, for once glued into position it will be very difficult to alter.

FIXING THE FRONTS

The piano hinges for the middle opening fronts should be cut to length and fixed in position with

FIG 21.20 *Fitting the porch columns and detail of column assembly*

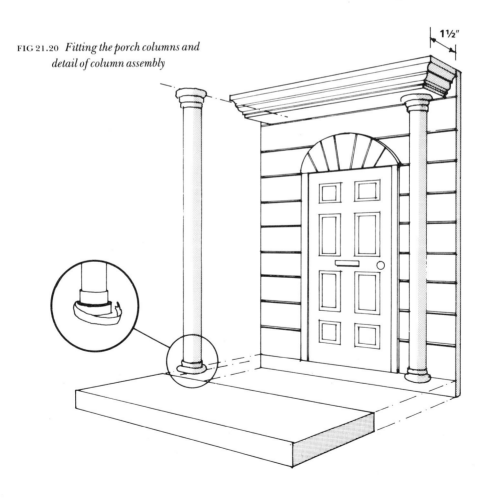

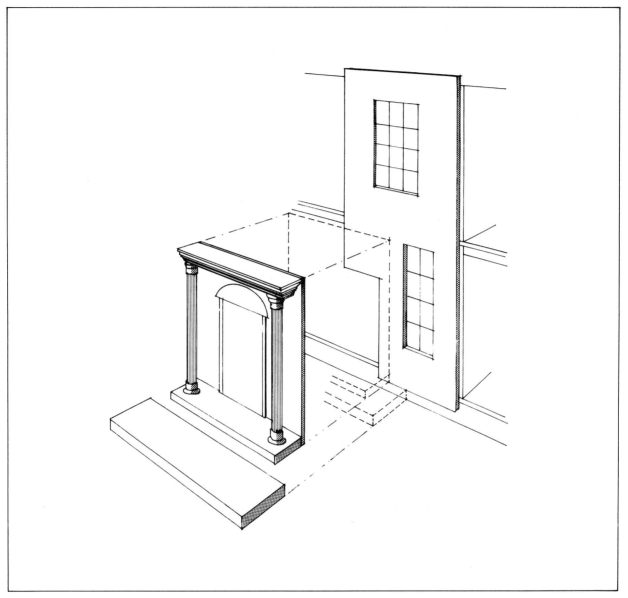

FIG 21.21 *Fitting the porch and step*

double-sided tape before being screwed. Fig 21.18 shows that, when hinging these fronts to the front facings, ¼″ (shown shaded on the diagram) must be left uncovered to allow the side fronts to close securely. You now have a choice for the finishing used for the side and rear walls. These can be finished as suggested earlier, as shown in the photographs or in any other method you choose.

(*See* Chapter 16.) If you wish to add gutterings and downspouts, these are described fully in Chapter 13 and should be added before you finish the roofing, and Chapter 12 has all the information you will need on slates and tiling.

I hope that you have as much pleasure in the building of this model as I had in the construction of the original!

POSTSCRIPT

*I*N THIS FOLLOW-UP to *Making Tudor Dolls'
Houses* it seemed logical to move on to the
Georgian and Regency periods of architecture,
when brick and stone were the main building
materials – this, of course, remains true of the vast
majority of buildings constructed to this day.

To enable me to cover the Tudor period in a
comprehensive manner, the book was dedicated
solely to that era. This decision was apparently the
right one, judging from the many letters I have
received congratulating me and the publishers for
taking that particular course rather than producing
a book that would cover a number of periods only
fleetingly.

The response to the Tudor book has encouraged
me to believe that to cover one period at a time as
comprehensively as possible is very rewarding –
not only to the reader, but also to myself as the
writer. Following this format, I am already formu-
lating a book on the Victorian and Edwardian eras,
where the problems of design and construction
techniques must again be addressed. After that – I
feel a line must be drawn.

Modelling all manner of subjects has over the
centuries held an irresistible fascination for craftsmen and artists, and house and furniture modelling
is no exception. Examples of older work have sur-
vived and some are available for viewing in
museums and galleries.

I hope that you found this book an enjoyable
read and that you may have found some inspiration
in it.

STOCKISTS
AND SUPPLIERS

TOOLS

BLACK & DECKER LIMITED (Minicraft Power Tools),
Westpoint, The Grove, Slough, Berks SL1 1QQ

COMO DRILLS,
Mill Lane, Worth, Deal, Kent CT14 0PA

FCA PRODUCTS,
First Floor, Unit One, 1–7 Bowman Trading
Estate, Westmoreland Road, Kingsbury, London
NW9

TIMBER MOULDINGS

BORCRAFT MINIATURES,
8 Fairfax View, Scotland Lane, Horsforth, Leeds,
W. Yorks LS18 5SZ

BLACKWELLS OF HAWKWELL,
733/5 London Road, Westcliff, Southend-on-Sea,
Essex SS0 9ST

DIJON (IMPORTERS) LIMITED,
Ashgrove, Cross-in-Hand, Heathfield, E. Sussex
TN21 0QG
(Trade only, but will let you know the nearest stockist)

WENTAWAY MINIATURES,
Wentaways, West End, Marden, Kent TN12 9JA

ROOFING MATERIALS AND BRICKS

SUSSEX CRAFTS,
6 Robinson Road, Crawley, W. Sussex RH11 7AB

DIJON (IMPORTERS) LIMITED *(see above)*

BLACKWELLS OF HAWKWELL *(see above)*

PLASTER MOULDINGS

RED HOUSE MINIATURES,
The Curatage, Warden, Nr. Hexham,
Northumberland NE46 4SS

LIGHTING AND ACCESSORIES

WOOD 'N' WOOL MINIATURES,
Yew Tree House, 3 Stankelt Road, Silverdale,
Carnforth, Lancs LA5 0RB

DIJON (IMPORTERS) LIMITED *(see above)*

DOORS AND WINDOWS

BORCRAFT MINIATURES *(see above)*

WENTAWAY MINIATURES *(see above)*

DIJON (IMPORTERS) LIMITED *(see above)*

BLACKWELLS OF HAWKWELL *(see above)*

STAIRS/BANNISTERS/POSTS ETC.

BORCRAFT MINIATURES *(see above)*

DIJON (IMPORTERS) LIMITED *(see above)*

SUSSEX CRAFTS *(see above)*

WENTAWAY MINIATURES *(see above)*

WALLPAPERS

SMALL INTERIORS,
3 Oakfield Street, London SW10 9JA

DIJON (IMPORTERS) LIMITED *(see above)*

FLOORS AND FLOORING EFFECT

BORCRAFT MINIATURES *(see above)*

SUSSEX CRAFTS *(see above)*

BLACKWELLS OF HAWKWELL *(see above)*

STAINED GLASS

WENTAWAY MINIATURES *(see above)*

FIREPLACES, GRATES ETC.

TONY HOOPER,
3 Bunting Close, Ogwell, Newton Abbot, Devon
TQ12 6BO

WOOD 'N' WOOL MINIATURES *(see above)*

DIJON (IMPORTERS) LIMITED *(see above)*

SUSSEX CRAFTS *(see above)*

HINGES, HANDLES ETC.

JOHN HODGSON,
25 Sands Lane, Bridlington, N. Humberside YO15 2JG

BLACKWELLS OF HAWKWELL *(see above)*

SUSSEX CRAFTS *(see above)*

DIJON (IMPORTERS) LIMITED *(see above)*

WENTAWAY MINIATURES *(see above)*

INDEX

ABOUT THE AUTHOR

DEREK ROWBOTTOM has been modelling since the age of 11, when he was confined to the house for a number of years with a very serious illness. Reading and modelling were his only pastimes, and modelling has remained his favourite occupation. A period at art college gave him an enthusiasm for painting old houses, and he began building them in earnest in 1980. His first book, *Making Tudor Dolls' Houses*, was published by GMC Publications in 1990. Examples of his work can be seen at miniaturist and dolls' house exhibitions around the country.

TITLES AVAILABLE FROM GMC PUBLICATIONS LTD

BOOKS

Woodworking Plans and Projects	GMC Publications	Making Dolls' House Furniture	Patricia King
40 More Woodworking Plans and Projects	GMC Publications	Making and Modifying Woodworking Tools	Jim Kingshott
Woodworking Crafts Annual	GMC Publications	The Workshop	Jim Kingshott
Woodworkers' Career and Educational Source Book	GMC Publications	Sharpening: The Complete Guide	Jim Kingshott
Woodworkers' Courses & Source Book	GMC Publications	Turning Wooden Toys	Terry Lawrence
Green Woodwork	Mike Abbott	Making Board, Peg and Dice Games	Jeff & Jennie Loader
Making Little Boxes from Wood	John Bennett	The Complete Dolls' House Book	Jean Nisbett
The Incredible Router	Jeremy Broun	Furniture Projects for the Home	Ernest Parrott
Electric Woodwork	Jeremy Broun	Making Money from Woodturning	Ann & Bob Phillips
Woodcarving: A Complete Course	Ron Butterfield	Members' Guide to Marketing	Jack Pigden
Making Fine Furniture: Projects	Tom Darby	Woodcarving Tools and Equipment	Chris Pye
Restoring Rocking Horses	Clive Green & Anthony Dew	Making Tudor Dolls' Houses	Derek Rowbottom
Heraldic Miniature Knights	Peter Greenhill	Making Georgian Dolls' Houses	Derek Rowbottom
Practical Crafts: Seat Weaving	Ricky Holdstock	Making Period Dolls' House Furniture	Derek & Sheila Rowbottom
Multi-centre Woodturning	Ray Hopper	Woodturning: A Foundation Course	Keith Rowley
Complete Woodfinishing	Ian Hosker	Turning Miniatures in Wood	John Sainsbury
Woodturning: A Source Book of Shapes	John Hunnex	Pleasure and Profit from Woodturning	Reg Sherwin
Making Shaker Furniture	Barry Jackson	Making Unusual Miniatures	Graham Spalding
Upholstery: A Complete Course	David James	Woodturning Wizardry	David Springett
Upholstery Techniques and Projects	David James	Furniture Projects	Rod Wales
Designing and Making Wooden Toys	Terry Kelly	Decorative Woodcarving	Jeremy Williams

VIDEOS

Dennis White Teaches Woodturning

Part 1	Turning Between Centres	**Jim Kingshott**	Sharpening The Professional Way
Part 2	Turning Bowls	**Ray Gonzalez**	Carving a Figure - the female form
Part 3	Boxes, Goblets and Screw Threads		
Part 4	Novelties and Projects		
Part 5	Classic Profiles		
Part 6	Twists and Advanced Turning		

GMC Publications regularly produces new books and videos on a wide range of woodworking and craft subjects, and an increasing number of specialist magazines, all available on subscription:

MAGAZINES

WOODCARVING   WOODTURNING   BUSINESSMATTERS

All these publications are available through bookshops and newsagents, or may be ordered by post from the publishers at 166 High Street, Lewes, East Sussex BN7 1XU, telephone (0273) 477374, fax (0273) 478606

Credit card orders are accepted. Please write or phone for the latest information